JOHN McEWEN:
RIGHT MAN, RIGHT PLACE, RIGHT TIME

BRIDGET McKENZIE

Connor Court

Published in 2020 by Connor Court Publishing Pty Ltd

Copyright © Bridget McKenzie

All rights reserved. No part of this book may be reproduced or transmitted in any form or by any means, electronic or mechanical, including photo copying, recording or by any information storage and retrieval system, without prior permission in writing from the publisher.

Connor Court Publishing Pty Ltd
PO Box 7257
Redland Bay QLD 4165
sales@connorcourt.com
www.connorcourt.com
Phone 0497-900-685

Printed in Australia

ISBN: 9781922449412

Front cover design: Maria Giordano

Front cover picture: William DARGIE {1912-2003)The Rt Hon. John McEwen, 1969, Parliament House Art Collection, Department of Parliamentary Services, Canberra, ACT. Used with Permission.

Cartoons used in this work have been used with permission.

I dedicate this book to my dear father, Neville Alan McKenzie, for being brave and honest; accepting and conservative; fair but flawed; a very decent, hardworking country Victorian. To thank him for always supporting me and for working so very hard to ensure I had every opportunity. I miss him every day.

CONTENTS

INTRODUCTION		7
1.	PROTECTIONIST OR PRAGMATIST?	11
2.	PLACE	35
3.	PARTY	51
4.	PATRIOT	69
5.	POWER	87
6.	PRIME MINISTER	121
7	THE NEW McEWENISTS	135
APPENDIX		149
ACKNOWLEDGEMENTS		169
ENDNOTES		159
INDEX		173

INTRODUCTION

"You can take the boy out of the country, but you can't take the country out of the boy." - Carl Perkins

John McEwen is a forgotten giant of Australian political history. Self-made, not born into privilege, his contribution across 37 years is unparalleled, laying the very foundations of modern Australia as a first world economy, and as an independent, sovereign power. And yet, McEwen rarely if ever features on even one powerpoint slide of an economics, international relations or political science lecture in our universities. Is this because he was from the Country Party, or simply because he was from the country?

Perhaps it is because McEwen was a pragmatist rather than an ideologue and his unfashionable practical form of economic management has been superseded by a prescriptive economic orthodoxy over the last 50 years. In this the centenary year of The Nationals, a statue of this political titan is rightfully being erected in Canberra. Finally, humble McEwen can stand straight and tall amongst the pantheon of the architects of our great nation, Barton, Deakin, Menzies, Curtin, and Chifley.

Physically, McEwen was a striking man. Six feet tall, with the straight bearing of a soldier on parade, square-jawed, with piercing crystal blue eyes that were so brilliantly captured by the artist Sir William Dargie in his official parliamentary portrait. This painting hangs in the Commonwealth Parliament alongside Australia's other prime ministers and captures not only McEwen's visionary gaze and the gnarled old hands of a farmer in his lap, but also his unflinching character.

The adjectives often used to describe McEwen can be contradictory. On the one side is the dour, choleric, incredibly determined and unyielding hard man of politics. On the other is the compassionate, patient, humorous, and generous mentor.

McEwen was indisputably a very serious man known for his stern outlook, dark often furrowed brow that seemed never to deviate and rarely to crack into a smile in public - even in photographs of the happy occasions of his youth. Such was his temperament that Menzies gave him his enduring moniker—'Black Jack'. His was an intelligent face, but a face that had also seen deprivation, great suffering and loss, the face of a workaholic, of single-mindedness, and of great physical pain in his later years.

The two personalities indeed seem difficult to reconcile. And yet the forging of these traits, with all their internal contradictions, in very poor circumstances in a small pocket of north eastern Victoria were the essential qualities that propelled McEwen to be a PM. These qualities made him able to reimagine a nation emerging from war to build entire industries from scratch, and to cleave Australia from the motherland England and carve a truly independent, sovereign vision for Australia.

These traits also enabled McEwen to stand up to powerful vested interests, to lead a minority to affect the majority, to guide an entire nation into the deepest of friendships with its most hated enemy, and to articulate such a clearly defined policy platform under his remit that it became synonymous with his own surname – *"McEwenism"*.

This book is intended to be a reintroduction to McEwen. It does not cover everything. It does not detail the man's important role in four of the most significant developments in Australian political history: his contribution to the founding of the United Nations in San Francisco with H.V. (Bert) Evatt and Frank Forde; nor McEwen's refusal of the United States' demand for the entire Aussie wool clip during the Korean War, bringing about the 1950s wool boom; it does not explain his 1939 White Paper on Aboriginal Australians which aimed to extend Australian citizenship; nor does it touch on his role in dismantling the White Australia policy and championing of a non-preferential immigration policy. This and more has had to be omitted. For a full-length biography, Peter Golding's book remains the gold standard. Instead, my little book reflects on six themes in the great man's life: Protectionist or Pragmatist?; Place, Party, Patriot, Power and Prime Minister.

Protectionist or Pragmatist? – he drove the economic and trade policy of *McEwenism*

Place - he was shaped by his local community and the natural environment

Party - he personified the Country Party, Australia's specialist regional political party

Patriot - he had a deep love for Australia, desired its sovereignty and security, serving it passionately

Power - he understood the need to acquire power, and wielded it, for a purpose

Prime Minister - he reached the highest office in Australian political for 23 days

This biography is not a chronological history of McEwen's life and contribution, rather it contains selected examples of deliberate actions and events that I hope will illustrate the man and his mission, and the role he played in Australia's growth and development during the twenty-first century. It is often too easy to look back on such great men with rose-coloured glasses, but this is not intended to be a hagiography.

Finally, aside from being a curiosity of history, what can we learn from McEwen today? Particularly as *McEwenism* has been derided by the Right and was dismantled by the Left. The final chapter examines this question. My hope is that this modest contribution will ignite interest in the man, his approach and the critical but unique role regional Australia and their political representatives have played in our national story.

Enjoy,

-- Senator The Hon. Bridget McKenzie

1
PROTECTIONIST OR PRAGMATIST?

"The strong do what they will and the weak suffer what they must" – Thucydides

It's 1957 and John McEwen is sitting on a plane next to Alan Westerman, one of his closest advisers. They take off, bound for Tokyo. As the surface of the Australian continent begins to slowly disappear from his view, what is going through 'Black Jack's' mind? Is he thinking back on his service on Curtin's War Advisory Council and the anxious planning of a desperate defence against the Japanese advance - that same nation with which he now seeks commercial and political partnership? Is he imagining the conversations in pubs up and down the country about this trip, or the motions of censure being passed against him in the RSL (Returned and Services League) clubs, in which horrific memories of the prisoner-of-war camps in Changi and on the Burma railway remained raw and real? In making this journey to forge a trade deal with Australia's erstwhile enemy, McEwen must know that he is putting everything on the line. Despite his moniker McEwen was never a gambler — but here he had gone all in on Japan, risking every chip of political capital that he had carefully accumulated over a lifetime on this one hand. All in against the House.

It is widely recognised that Australia's trade deal with Japan is McEwen's greatest achievement in a long and illustrious career. However, at the time, his colleagues thought McEwen was at best destroying his own career and at worst committing treason. Malcolm Fraser, then a young MP, remembered that McEwen threatened to personally campaign in the electorates of any Liberal MPs who publicly undermined the deal.[1] Nevertheless, McEwen took full ownership of the negotiations and agreed to shouldering all of the predicted public backlash, labelling the Japan deal in interviews as 'my policy', never 'the Government's policy'. Reflecting on it he wrote, "(m)*y friends knew that I was making sure that, if I were to fall on this, the Government would not have to fall with me. In other words, I was willing to carry the political responsibility for the treaty on my own. As I remember, no-one else was keen to share the burden of carrying it*".[2] According to Fraser, McEwen was friendless in Cabinet and Menzies, though he allowed the negotiations to proceed, forbade it being done in the name of the Government. "*So the risk was McEwen's,*" said Fraser, "*that was the measure of the greatness of the man.*"[3] The Labor Party, led by H.V. Evatt, opposed the deal running predictable lines at the dispatch box about cheap Japanese imports flooding the Australian market and putting Australian workers out of a job. But McEwen understood that more open trade would lead to more jobs for Australians and this was the hill he was prepared to die on.

It seems like a contradiction that the greatest legacy of an ostensible arch-protectionist is the normalising of Australia's trade relations with Japan. The apparent paradox is striking. For the Japanese, this trade deal with Australia was seen at the time (and it is a view that history vindicates) as a crucial first step in reentering the 'community of nations,' allowing Japan to be a part of the great new peaceful era of freer international trade after World War Two. By 1962 the Australia-Japan Business Cooperation Committee was formed; by 1966 it was proposing a Pacific Basin trade forum, an APEC (Australian-Pacific Economic Cooperation) precursor; by 1970, Japan was seeking to lead a Japan Round of GATT (General Agreement on Tariffs and Trade) negotiations to slash tariffs. On the Australian side, McEwen's deal would make Japan our biggest trading partner for decades, and while China now boasts that accolade, it is fair, in light of recent difficulties, to say that even today Japan remains our 'closest' trading partner. In 2014, former prime ministers Tony Abbott and Shinzo Abe signed a comprehensive Free Trade Agreement, which was the culmination of McEwen's courageous first step nearly 60 years earlier. Every day, the fruits of this trading relationship are personally experienced by citizens of both nations – after all, 90 per cent of Port Lincoln tuna catch ends up in the Tokyo Fish Markets and in Australia we are a nation of Toyota Hilux drivers. And somehow all of this ultimately stemmed from the vision of one of the so-called great arch-protectionists in Australian political history. It doesn't seem to make much sense. Completing the paradox, the most vicious attacks against McEwen for the Japan deal did not end up coming from the RSL whose membership was surprisingly philosophical about it, nor from Labor, but from the Australian manufacturing sector.

When most Australian economists and politicians hear the dreaded P word, 'protectionism,' typically their imaginations conjure nightmares of wasting millions in propping up a non-competitive car manufacturing industry. Ultimately, they tell us, it is the Aussie consumer that ends up having to pay for really expensive cars for the sake of an irrational exercise in jingoism. And, guess what, they are right. But if this is protectionism, then, as the Japan deal shows, it is fair to say that McEwen was never philosophically an absolute protectionist.

McEwenism was about nation-building — taking a small Dominion on a great ancient continent, hitherto riding on the sheep's back, and transforming it into a modern, industrialised, independent sovereign power. McEwen established lucrative new export markets for our commodity producers and, yes, the wealth this generated paid for the preservation of the tariff walls that protected our nascent manufacturing sector. But McEwen championed 'Protection for All'. It meant that primary industry also got protection, because, in McEwen's words, *"efficient primary production requires long-term investment and planning"* and so it needed to offer *"a reasonable prospect of profit"*[4] for the hopeful farmer who has the guts to have a go. McEwen managed to sustain Australian tariffs, and those of other middle powers, at the GATT negotiations in face of enormous international pressure to lower them. In his final years in politics, McEwen is the man who fought tooth and nail against the Tariff Board's Alf Rattigan, who sought to begin winding protection back. Rattigan managed it in dramatic fashion not long after McEwen retired when self-described "Rattigan man"[5] Gough Whitlam unilaterally in 1973 reduced all tariffs by 25 per cent in one go, to disastrous consequences. It is easy to assume based on all this, as historian Andrew Black recounts, that for McEwen the tariff was *"an article of faith"*.⁶ The inimitable Paul Kelly has similarly written that McEwen's all-round protection was *"not just a political strategy; it was a faith."*⁷

But those who knew and worked with McEwen categorically, to a man, disagree with this assessment. Yes, the tariff was a tool that McEwen valued, but neither did he worship at its altar. It was a means to an end. Indeed, former Country Party Minister Peter Nixon says that history has misremembered McEwen's trade philosophy. *"McEwen was wise enough to know, and he would have changed as the world changed,"* Nixon says on tariffs. *"It's something people never understand. He was far sighted. He'd look ahead to see what the storms were and he'd be ready to meet them."*⁸ Sir John Crawford, McEwen's Trade Department head, said, *"...(McEwen) recognised in later years that the growing complexity of the economy demanded rather more careful assessment of the tariff structure; in short that there were costs (often affecting our export industries) to be assessed as well as possible gains (e.g. to employment) to be recorded."*⁹ And as international trade expert Colin Teese recognised, *"(McEwen) believed in market capitalism as the superior form of economic organisation, though not in the infallibility of markets."*¹⁰

McEwen had none of the negative hallmarks of a stereotypical doctrinaire protectionist, being neither parochial nor isolationist. In many ways McEwen was a progressive and an outward-looking person. McEwen was a trader. In his private business as a farmer he relished the buying and selling of goods and he had a reputation as a hard-nosed negotiator. Even as a working politician, rarely did a day pass without McEwen having a flick through the classifieds in search of a bargain piece of equipment for his farm. He may have been 'Black Jack' in Canberra, but on his property, *Chilgala*, among the farmhands, he was known as 'Secondhand Jack'. McEwen would not tolerate being ripped off in any deal. It was this traders/dealmaker single-mindedness that he brought to Geneva's *Palais des Nations* in international trade negotiations on behalf of a burgeoning Australia.

McEwen appreciated the efficiencies of freer trade and he was a supporter of all nations lowering their tariffs at the GATT, but McEwen did not believe that a 'flat earth' vision of completely open trade was either realistic or ultimately a good thing for Australians. Simply, McEwen was a Realist. He consistently argued that while the leaders of nations may espouse a grand doctrine of an open world and a 'level playing field', when push came to shove, they would ruthlessly act in the interests of their own nations. In a 1962 speech to a meeting of the Australian Club in London, McEwen articulated this world-view well:

> *I have said previously with perhaps a tinge of bitterness that what is doctrinally pure in trade when enunciated from Washington happens in application to be advantageous to American interests. Finally, America and Britain and Germany and Japan will do what best suits their own interests. They will respond to their own domestic pressures.*[11]

All politics is local.

The Kennedy Round

McEwen was more than a little sceptical of multilateral trading arrangements, understanding that they favoured the large, already industrialised first world economies of the United States (US), Britain and the emerging European bloc. The Kennedy Round (1964-67) was one of the great international trading conferences of the 20th century, and its aim was a 50 per cent reduction in tariffs for all GATT nations. McEwen did not disagree with the core principle of freer and more predictable trade,[12] but knew that the tariff reduction represented a *"considerable threat to Australia's interests,"*[13] and a much worse threat to even more underdeveloped economies. This was because commodities, which we did well at, were already largely globally traded without barriers, whereas manufacturing, in which we were only beginning to see success, was where all the tariffs would come down. In other words, while Australian consumers might have seen some economic benefit from the broad liberalisation, Australian producers would gain nothing, and our adolescent industry would be prematurely exposed. During the negotiations McEwen brought together the delegations of South Africa and New Zealand and personally carved out an exemption for these middle nations and the even more underdeveloped nations such as Brazil, Pakistan, Greece, Peru, Nicaragua, and the French African colonies. McEwen made himself a *"champion of the secondary powers,"* stating, *"there is nothing we are fighting for on Australia's behalf which we are not equally fighting for on behalf of all the young countries of the world"*.[14] He brought to Geneva the lessons of collective bargaining he learnt from rural life, agri-politics, and competing sectional interests.

The finale of the Kennedy Round is a demonstration of McEwen's astonishing strength of character. The great conference, which had lasted for three long years, was entering its final session, which was supposed to be just a formality in celebration of the universal resolution that had been achieved. The session was due to begin at five o'clock but at two minutes to five the New Zealand delegate informed McEwen that the European Group had recanted on its agreement for exemption for Australia, South Africa and New Zealand. The decision, McEwen was told, had been ratified by the various European ministers who had now gone home to their respective countries and so the decision could not be changed. Resolute, McEwen didn't budge, and debate raged late into the night. The New Zealand and South African ministers were unable to be there to help McEwen and notably Britain offered no help at all. McEwen eventually told the conference that Australia would sooner leave the GATT than agree to the terms offered. When it became clear that the GATT project itself was at risk, the other nations found a backdoor way to reinstate the exemption status. The world waited for McEwen.

McEwen had attended many of these international conferences in his career and he became acutely aware of the propensity of big nations to bully smaller ones. Instead of these conglomerate institutions, McEwen believed that fair, mutually beneficial bilateral partnerships were the best vehicle for secure and predictable trade between nations. Most of all, McEwen disagreed vehemently with Free Trade acolytes who advocated Australia unilaterally reduce tariffs. McEwen sought a more sophisticated approach to tariffs, selectively reducing them for specific nations that wanted to export to Australia, but not without first achieving offsets of strategic value from them in return. Country Party Minister Ralph Hunt once recalled McEwen's astonishing reaction to a trade report he had worked on with a well-known Free Trade advocate, Senator Tom Bull. According to Hunt, when he handed his leader the report, McEwen read no further than the executive summary before tearing it up and throwing it in the bin. Hunt remembered McEwen saying that he had fought - indeed nobody had fought harder than he — to reduce global tariffs at the GATT. However, seeing as the other nations had refused to reduce protection on key industries, McEwen was not about to put Australian industry at a competitive disadvantage by reducing protection unilaterally.

It is easy to forget just how different the post-war world was to today. It was a world of Bretton Woods, the gold standard, and fixed exchange rates. Most importantly, there was no World Trade Organisation (WTO). Rarely is McEwen given the benefit of being judged as a man of his time. What did McEwen try to protect Australia's infant industry from? *"What's been lost in the debate is dumping,"* Peter Nixon explains, *"A hell of a lot of countries in those days were over-manufacturing and dumping. We were always within the world trade rules with our operations"*.[15]

The original GATT condemned dumping, but it did not prohibit it. As Professor Kym Anderson says, dispute resolution processes were, *"toothless really until the WTO"*.[16] The GATT did allow countries to implement countermeasures such as quotas or tariffs. It is easy to criticise *McEwenism* from the privileged position of the contemporary rules-based framework (that he helped construct) where we are protected by a WTO that has a well-developed framework to address claims of dumping. However, in McEwen's time, the threat of dumping was all too real and would destroy Australian companies and put people out of work. On the other hand, it would be slightly revisionist to say McEwenist protection was exclusively about anti-dumping.

Protectionism, in truth, was ubiquitous right across the political spectrum at the time.[17] *"He was a terrible protectionist, but of course everyone was a protectionist,"* said John Howard of McEwen, *"you've got to understand that. Everyone was"*.[18] Even Howard, the great Liberal reformer, admits that he was much more protectionist when he was Malcolm Fraser's Treasurer. Protection was one of the tenets of the Federation Trifecta — as formulated by Gerard Henderson — the tripart legacy of Alfred Deakin that was forged in collaboration with the Labor Party.[19] The other two pillars of this bipartisan legacy were the White Australia policy and centralised industrial relations. Under Harold Holt Australian immigration was being liberalised and importantly the White Australia policy effectively dismantled; under Bob Hawke protection of industry was removed; and Howard as prime minister had a go at liberalising labour laws especially during his fourth and last term. But in the 1950s, none of these three pillars were fundamentally contested in the mainstream of either side of politics and they broadly had the full support of the electorate. As Howard told me, *"I am a great supporter of Menzies, but he thought the Arbitration Commission was terrific!"*[20]

Interestingly, the notable exception to the consensus on these policy areas was actually the Country Party in which there was traditionally a powerful voice advocating for Free Trade. In the NSW division especially, which is grazier territory, there were frequent calls in the 1960s for a reform of our approach to tariffs. In 1990, Peter Golding discussed this with Sir John Fuller, a member of the federal executive and NSW chairman of the Country Party. Fuller recalled that there were annual arguments on tariffs and that *"John McEwen always won but it was often after a very good discussion"*.[21] The graziers in his own party were pressuring McEwen for freer trade in a way that was not yet occurring in either the Labor or Liberal parties.

But McEwen was from Victoria, the manufacturing state and home to the soldier settler, and so there were other political considerations to weigh up. Demographics were changing, and just like today, relatively less and less people were living in rural areas, threatening to diminish the Country Party's influence. At the same time, manufacturers who benefited from McEwen's tariff wall were emerging as prominent donors to the Country Party.

So, this was John McEwen's world. He was the leader of the only political party that had any serious advocates for Free Trade, but was also from the manufacturing state in which there were perhaps the most vociferous supporters of his *'protection for all'* policy. More importantly, Australia was a sparsely populated nation emerging from World War Two as a middle power with fragile infant industries, and McEwen had to represent that nation during the bold new multilateral era of the UN (United Nations) and the GATT in which the great powers sought a global reduction in tariffs. In the midst of all of this, McEwen could not afford to have a rigidly ideological approach to trade whether that was as an arch-protectionist or Free Trade absolutist. He had to be pragmatic and tough. That suited him just fine.

Why McEwenism?

Some of his critics have claimed that McEwen's trade policies were entirely cynical, serving merely to expand his own power base. There is no denying that McEwen, as in Paul Keating's words "*gripped the flame of power and held on,*"[22] but if he only cared about power for its own sake then he would have left the Country Party at any number of points. McEwen was ambitious but he was not selfish; he had an enormous capacity for empathy and was driven primarily by what he saw as his duty to serve. Nor was *McEwenism* merely pragmatism and tough negotiating. *McEwenism* was a coherent philosophy founded on its author's most deeply held moral convictions. The pillars of McEwen's 'framework' were full employment, wage maintenance, support for manufacturing, population growth and greater self-sufficiency. In the term *'protection for all'* it was the *'for all'* part that was most important to McEwen. McEwen believed that greater efficiency should not be the sole objective of governments and that economic growth must be accompanied by fairness. In essence, McEwen's entire career boiled down to two core objectives — securing full employment and defending national sovereignty. It was these two objectives that underpinned the whole of the great man's life in office.

These are not unique goals for a politician to strive for - the post-war Chifley Labor Government released in 1945 an important White Paper, *Full Employment in Australia* — but what was unique was the intensity of McEwen's devotion to the two causes. There is little else that ever held his attention for long.

McEwen's obsession with unemployment came primarily from Place — his experiences in the destitution of his post-war youth and later during the Great Depression. As an 18-year-old McEwen was a poor orphaned boy with nothing but an 86 acre rabbit infested block to his name. Despite no farming experience, McEwen found he had a knack for it. Many of his fellow soldier-settlers fared much worse. Young McEwen had many friends and neighbours who had fought at Gallipoli or on the Western Front who lived their lives in complete poverty and desperation. McEwen never forgot the sight of soldier-settlers selling sheep for barely more than what it cost to get them to market. There was one particular memory that would bring McEwen to tears years later when he recalled it. One of his neighbours, *"a typical hard-working, hard-bitten Australian with a good heart"* was forced to dig a grave for his little child because he could not afford a funeral. *"Next year,"* McEwen recollected *"the government put that soldier off his land because he couldn't pay"*.[23] It was these memories that drove McEwen. These were his people; he was one of them. He wanted to help them, and he believed the best way to do it was by creating secure jobs, and this meant Australia needed industry. McEwen came to see trade policy as the key lever to achieve the industrialisation he believed was the only way to create the quantity and quality of jobs that Australia needed. In addition to this moral imperative, McEwen also argued that the cost of protecting job-creating industry would ultimately be less than the financial burden for governments that is created by widespread unemployment.

As for McEwen's concern over national defence, it similarly stemmed from lived experience. It was an enormous shock to McEwen how unprepared Australia was to confront the Japanese attack. Shaken first by the events in the South Pacific in the early years of the war, the young Minister for Air was horrified at the prospect of bright-eyed young Australian airmen boarding the little fleet of Wirraways he had helped cobble together to go toe-to-toe with the mighty Japanese Zeros. In Peter Golding's eloquent words:

> *(A)s a member of the War Advisory Council he read daily bulletins of the southward thrust of the Japanese forces, bombs falling on Darwin, Japanese mini-submarines in Sydney Harbour and the epic struggles in New Guinea. The need for Australia to have the strongest possible defence capability was ingrained in the man. McEwen had an absolute conviction that the world would not allow a handful of Australians — about 7 million at the time - to occupy such a vast rich continent; that indeed it was immoral to do so.*[24]

It was because of this that McEwen believed Australia needed to increase its population, but he simultaneously was challenged by the fact that high immigration may endanger full employment. All of this again reinforced McEwen in his view on retaining 'protection for all'. As Nixon recalled:

> *He* (McEwen) *believed that the tariffs granted were too high. What used to happen, a company would be given tariff protection and then the unions would squeeze the company for higher wages. What people don't understand is that when the war finished, we had migrants pouring into the country that had to be employed. There was a hell of a strong trade union movement in those days. In those days, anybody who worked anywhere was a trade unionist. And so, we had a high wage level compared to our competitors internationally. Tariffs were the answer. And sometimes the unions would strike for a wage rise and that was granted by the wage body at the time and that would put the damn industry at risk.*[25]

For McEwen self-sufficiency was the key driver post war, a policy objective driven not by the ideology of protectionism as an article of faith, rather as a pragmatic response to real world issues. As former Victorian Nationals Deputy Premier Pat McNamara has said *"as a senior person in the government saying the country needs to be more self-sufficient. I don't think it would have been an ideological thing; I think it's a practical thing"*.[26]

***

The Secretaries: Crawford and Westerman

It is important to analyse McEwen's two departmental secretaries Sir John Crawford and Sir Alan Westerman. In a way, these two men represent two important sides to McEwen's character and their influence on his trade policies should not be understated.

Crawford was, by all accounts, a calm, scholarly type, and a truly brilliant economic thinker. He came to the public service from an academic background, educated in the school of Australia's first Keynesians: Giblin, Brigden, Copland, Mills, Mauldon and Shann.[27] Edward Shann in particular had significant influence on this period, his students also including Sir Paul Hasluck and the other great public servant Nugget Coombs, although by his own admission, Crawford was much less of a free trader than Shann. Most importantly, like McEwen, Crawford was a great visionary. Crawford believed that good trade relations would lead to peaceful political relations between nations. He advocated from as early as the 1930s that Australia should look outside of Britain to the Far East (or the Near North as Crawford thought we should call it) to expand our export markets, and specifically argued that Japan would not be so aggressive if the West included it more in international trade. On trade policy, McEwen and Crawford were simpatico, so much so that both Crawford and McEwen believed that they were directing the policy views of the other.[28] It was these two men, Crawford and McEwen, who finally broke Australia from the yoke of Britain and the Ottawa Agreement, economically reorienting the country towards opportunities in Asia; more on this later. What Crawford and McEwen shared was a vision and spirit of nation building.

Crawford was a thinker and McEwen a doer and together they were devastating. McEwen knew it. He had handpicked Crawford to be his department secretary for Primary Industry and kept him on to build a world class Trade and Industry department. Crawford's return to the academy in 1960 was a great loss, personally and professionally for McEwen. Crawford gave an interesting lecture in 1968 at the University of Western Australia. In it, Crawford defended the pragmatic approach that he and McEwen had taken together, and he also defended protection policies as temporarily necessary to get industry going. Like McEwen, Crawford appreciated the efficiencies of free trade, but believed Australia first needed to industrialise behind a protective wall before steadily pursuing these efficiencies with certain carefully selected complementary economies:

> *There are many economists and businessmen in Japan, and some in Australia, who foresee a free trade area relationship between Australia and Japan and other countries, especially North America and the United Kingdom. I do not see this as an early likelihood at*

> all. Australia is not ready for it; nor is Japan ready to dismantle its highly protective system applying to agriculture and, for example, to its own motor-vehicle industry. I do see sense and profit in both countries beginning to reduce tariff and non-tariff barriers against each other on an item-by-item basis.[29]

The key words here are *"Australia is not ready for it"*. The objective then is clear, to 'get Australia ready for it'.

Crawford's replacement, Alan Westerman was of a different ilk — a hard man, but rigorous and immensely competent. Like McEwen, he was a tough and persistent negotiator. It is Westerman who should get a lot of the credit for hammering out many of the finer details of the Japan deal, much of which was done in smoky Canberra motel rooms. According to Peter Nixon, *"Alan Westerman was one of the top public servants in the country"*.[30] McEwen also praised Westerman, once writing that he was a *"magnificent adviser who was very easy to work with."* This view is contested. John Stone, one time 'Joh for Canberra' senator and a high-ranking Treasury official in the 60s, and later Secretary of Treasury, has a very different perspective, *"There's no word for Westerman other than bastard"*.[31] Stone didn't elaborate on this except to say that both Crawford and Westerman were 'politician-public servants'. Journalist Maximillian Walsh once wrote:

> *Westerman survived and prospered because he was under the patronage of 'Black Jack' McEwen. Westerman had many successes as permanent head of the Department of Trade. His greatest triumph in personal terms was the drawing up, under his discretion, of the legislation*

> to establish the Australian Industries Development Corporation; then, having shepherded the project through Parliament, he resigned from the Department and became the first chairman of the Corporation.[32]

Westerman himself claimed that McEwen, "*was not a rabid protectionist ... he believed in it as a last resort, that there was no such thing as a 'level playing field' and that it never did or could exist. Therefore, there had to be some intervention in any so-called 'free market'*".[33] Again, McEwen approached Australia's engagement in the international trading system realistically and pragmatically, with a trader's instinct, unconstrained by any prescriptive textbook. In that, McEwen and Westerman differed. Golding suggested McEwen was "*an interventionist by necessity, and Westerman by nature*".[34] But what is clear is that Westerman shared McEwen's ambition and his ruthlessness.

Changing Times and the Tariff Board

As the 1960s progressed, McEwen became more intransigent about 'protection for all' just as others outside of the Country Party were beginning to pick up the 'free trade' cause. McEwen may not have been the PM, but he was the most senior man in government and so perhaps defending his policies became as much about protecting his own power as the outcomes that he strove for. Increasingly, prominent voices in Treasury and in the media, began suggesting that once necessary levels of protection were now propping up inefficient industry, but McEwen was reluctant to begin the process of winding back industry assistance. Golding questioned whether McEwen, without Crawford by his side, was being badly advised, or whether as he got older, he was just becoming 'pig headed'. Certainly, the narrative of this period has been drastically oversimplified, with all the nuances ironed out, leaving us with the picture of the old arch-protectionist holding out against Young Turk economic rationalists. As Professor Peter Drysdale, who went on radio at the time to defend Gough Whitlam's *carte blanche* 25 per cent tariff reductions, has said,

> *"it is difficult to understand how these epithets get attached to people, except you know, back in the heat of the political battle about the particular issues of the day. There was a nest of those extremists in the Treasury and in the press, Maxwell Newton. They were kind of on the right side of history but their perceptions of their opponents at that time did not concede to them where they had come from and what they had done".*[35]

Perspective is everything. As Kym Anderson said *"from the point of view of that era* (the Ottawa Agreement era) *you would think of Westerman and Crawford as liberalisers. If you look at it from today's perspective, as economists, you would say they were reluctant liberalisers really".*[36] The same applies to McEwen. At the time he brought bold new ideas to our economy, that looking back seem now to be outdated.

Late in 1962, Sir Leslie Melville quit as the chairman of the Tariff Board, the statutory body in charge of industry assistance. Melville went on to take up a position in the World Bank, his quarrel with McEwen was not on the level of protection but rather on the independence of the Board. Nevertheless, it was not a good portent of events to come.[37] McEwen then appointed one of his Trade and Industry public servants Alf Rattigan, citing his competence and perhaps because he thought he would be easier to deal with than Melville. It was a mistake, because as the decade passed, Rattigan came to believe that McEwen was keeping industry protection measures too high and that Australia as a GATT nation was not doing enough for its part to reduce global trade barriers. But there is nuance. As one of McEwen's loyal public servants, Rattigan understood what *McEwenism* had accomplished. For example, in Rattigan's memoirs he outlined that until his appointment to the Tariff Board, Australia reduced customs tariffs selectively in bilateral negotiations in order to get reductions in barriers for our commodity exports and that McEwen had kept their level high as a tool to diversify the economy, protecting it from shocks.[38] As Golding states:

> ... neither Melville nor Rattigan, both arch critics of McEwen's protectionism, dismissed the need for some protection. So, when should the easing back have started? The consensus seems to be 1960 or at least the early 1960s, up till then protection was fine. The priority was to get manufacturing going again after the war to provide jobs for the hundreds of thousands of migrants pouring into the country but by the early 1960s Australia's manufacturing was expanding and becoming more competitive.[39]

As John Anderson says, "it is a bit like raising a child, at some point you have to let him go and make his own way".[40] Rattigan believed that McEwen's failure to begin this process of winding back protection was creating inefficiencies and holding back standards of living. Courageously, in 1970 Rattigan took McEwen on and proposed a review into the tariff structure.

The Age beautifully captured this moment:

> *There is something almost heroic in the posture of that grand old warrior, Sir John McEwen, rising on the eve of his retirement to strike out against the Tariff Board and on the eve of the important cabinet meeting on the economy calling on his ministerial colleagues to help him bring it under control. With his superb sense of timing and uncanny flair for the dramatic, he has contrived to project an image of the Tariff Board as a dangerous creature which, rebelling against the guidelines and unleashed from the restraints he has so far managed to impose upon it, is threatening to claw down the peaks of tariff protection and thus to 'jeopardise the livelihood of one fifth of the Australian population.' The emotion-packed impact has been heightened by the Associated Chamber of Manufactures, wailing like a Greek chorus of impending doom and imploring their knight-protector to remain at his post until the rampaging board is firmly locked into its cage of safe government restriction.* [41]

Journalists such as Maxwell Newton were launching attacks on *McEwenisim*. Rattigan had cultivated relationships within the press gallery to assist his cause of tariff reform, helping them with information whilst McEwen sought to block them. It was the rise of advocacy journalism that drove the public agenda during the debate regarding tariff policy in Australia. This ultimately saw significant changes to the level of support for the 'protection for all' policies of McEwen.[42] In 1971, the Cabinet agreed to a review of the levels of protection for manufacturing industries and McEwen left the room "visibly upset".[43] One of McEwen's final acts as Minister was to sign off on a review of tariff settings as Rattigan had suggested. He retired within months.

And yet, however maligned it may be today, in its time and context, *McEwenism* worked. Australia at the end of the World War Two was poor, underdeveloped and reliant on the United Kingdom (UK). The partnership and policies of McEwen and Menzies drove a golden era of enormous egalitarian prosperity, affluence and opportunity. McEwen's Australia had a growing population, full employment, a diversified economy, no inflation, a decreasing debt and no balance of payments problems. McEwen's policies both achieved real returns for farmers and industrialised our hitherto immature economy. He took us off the teat of Britain and we grew up, finding new economic opportunities in Asia. In short, McEwen laid the foundations for us to become the independent G20 nation we are today. As public servant Sir Eric McLintock has said, *"given that he is regarded as such a stuff up, he was around in pretty good times. We should hire him back"*. [44] Paul Kelly, never one to resile from being a champion for global free trade, summed up McEwen's achievement like this:

> *He was gaunt, gigantic. An old-fashioned Australian who embodied some of the older virtues - courage, vision, pitiless determination. More influential than most of the prime ministers he served, Sir John McEwen was a cunning manipulator whose scale of operation encompassed the central elements in the Australian economy. McEwen is a forgotten figure: the ghost of an older age before vacuous lucidity became the test for the television politicians. But it is McEwen's imprint which remains indelible upon the nation today. The economic structures created by post World War Two governments were carved by McEwen. Not Menzies,*

Holt or Gorton. They were merely the Liberal prime ministers he served and who in turn impinged upon but never challenged his own economic domain.[45]

"Privatise the profits - and socialise the losses" [Black Jack's gospel of the Australian wheat industry] [picture] / Pryor

McCrae, Stewart. (1963). "Let's take a risk for peace! Ring the President for a definite date for our withdrawal!" [Amidst the Morgan Gallop polls and subsequent anti-war rallies throughout Australia in 1970, the Australian government began withdrawing troops from Vietnam; John Gorton became Liberal leader and Prime Minister, taking over from caretaker Prime Minister John McEwen] Retrieved November 27, 2020, from http://nla.gov.au/nla.obj-145851134

2
PLACE

"But the bush hath moods and changes, as the seasons rise and fall,

And the men who know the bush-land — they are loyal through it all."

- Banjo Paterson - In Defence of the Bush

To fully explore John McEwen, you must understand what growing up in the country means. Living your life in a rural community gifts a unique perspective that is denied to city people. Wide landscapes, harsh seasons, homogenous social structures, a combination of both resilience and independence and interdependence, together make life in the country different.

Farming has a moral purpose, underpinned by the earthy virtues of 'hard yakka' and deeply connected community. This is the Jeffersonian agrarian myth embodied by the characteristics of *"honor, manliness, self-reliance, courage, moral integrity, and hospitality"*[46] that epitomise rural men and women. "(T)hose who labour in the earth are the chosen people of God, if ever he had a chosen people".[47]

The 'moral purpose' of farming may be contestable, but the kernel of the myth, the importance of Place and 'countrymindedness' is apposite for John McEwen, Australia's 18th prime minister.

Despite the larger physical landscape, a person in a country town occupies a greater proportion of space because they are recognised by more people in the community. Living in a city there is no recollection of the people walked past, let alone waved to; there is no collective memory of such challenges as fighting fires together or the shared teaching of their children. With that social recognition comes greater responsibility and accountability to the community itself, an inbuilt stability. For those who are living on and earning a living from the land, the richness and quality of life stems from the isolation and therefore greater independence. Tragedy and triumph are also shared experiences in the country. If the local cricket club wins the district grand final, the community celebrates. Similarly, funerals are attended not just by close relatives, but the whole community mourns together. Changes in seasons have a greater impact both on income and daily social life. Country communities were typically homogenous, with social, economic and family ties more likely to be localised, with foundation institutions being footy clubs, the church, the Lodge, the Country Women's Association and the Country Party. People in the country don't rush to change for its own sake, hence tend towards classical conservatism. Yet threats from the outside be they people, policies or politicians are often met with collective resistance.

For McEwen three rural places, their natural environment, social institutions, and economic structures, were imprinted indelibly into his identity; they drove his politics and provided a touchstone. Chiltern's exciting industriousness as a mining town and his relative financial security; Wangaratta as an agricultural centre, which he recalls as a stable community; the Stanhope dairy district where so many of his fellow farmers endured unnecessary hardship. McEwen worked hard to build a successful farming enterprise and was never happier than when he was in the paddock or at the saleyard. It is no exaggeration to say that McEwen took these Places with him to Canberra and eventually the world.

McEwen was not born a farmer; he made a conscious decision to become one. He started from nothing, without family support, succeeding only through his wits and will. He delighted in farming's fickleness and joys. At a very young age McEwen experienced how the caprice of government policy, for good or ill, could profoundly affect the lives of men and women of rural Australia. So, when McEwen became a politician, he did not merely 'represent' the country, his politics were not abstract or academic - he was very much *of* the country with every fibre of his being. He had lived in the bustling industriousness of mining towns. He had worked among the soldier settlers, who had fought for their country in the First World War, but so many of whom were tragically too ill-equipped, inexperienced or poorly funded to make a survivable living out their tiny blocks. Through sheer determination, extraordinary hard work and innate acumen McEwen made his farm a success. He had cleared the ancient stones and stumps of his own soldier settler block with his bare hands. He had fenced paddocks, harvested grain, shorn the flock and built a herd. He had survived on literally nothing but the rabbits he shot, skinned and stewed. McEwen the political titan, who would be feared and respected by his political friends and foes in Australia in trade and political circles around the world, was born of Place.

Chiltern

McEwen deeply cherished the farm that he had built it up for more than half a century, but he perhaps had even greater affection for the place where he was born and lived till his seventh year. That place was Chiltern, a little town that sits 20-odd kilometres south of the Murray River in northeast Victoria.

Jack McEwen was born at the turn of the 19th century at *Linden*, a relatively stately brick home his father David had built for Jack's mother in 1890. *Linden* is still standing on one of Chiltern's two main streets, opposite the local Masonic Lodge and is an elegant local example of the architecture of the era. Chiltern is now a small village of just 1,600 people, but in its gold rush heyday Chiltern was a sight to behold. Boasting a population of over 20,000 people, it had rows of early Victorian shopfronts along a wide verandaed main street with 32 pubs to quench the industrious miners' thirsts. It was quite the hub.

Chiltern was the place where McEwen lived during his crucial formative years. It never left him, nor he it.

McEwen later recalled:

> *Whilst I remember Melbourne being slower than it has now become. I have a vivid memory of Chiltern being a very busy, bustling town, sleepy though it is now. Chiltern was never a big place — there were a dozen or so shops at the most — but, being a mining town, it was always full of life. People worked a six-day week then, there were four or five hotels opened from six in the morning until eleven at night. And in the mining community there was a tremendous bustle and business. For instance, on Saturday night, which was the night for shopping, a vehicle could not possibly get down the main street which was entirely crowded with people. That is my memory of Chiltern in 1907.*[48]

Perhaps John McEwen the child, watched this scene from the porch of his father's dispensary before being shooed to bed on a Saturday night. McEwen's father David was an Irish Presbyterian originally from Armagh, the ecclesiastical capital of Ireland, and the son of three generations of Presbyterian ministers. After arriving in Australia, he moved to Chiltern where he set up shop as the local pharmacist. David McEwen also became a Shire councillor and was widely respected for his educated perspective and regarded as an accomplished man of significance to the town. The *Federal Standard* newspaper's obituary extolled that David McEwen, Grand Master of the Lodge, was a great contributor to the town "the soul of geniality itself".[49]

Amy Ellen, nee Porter, (John McEwen's mother) was David's second wife. Amy, his second wife, died when John was just 18 months old — a loss McEwen claims in his memoirs, without a hint of irony, *"didn't perturb him"*.[50] On the other hand, the unexpected passing of his father when John was just seven, affected him greatly, according to the same memoirs. One day his Dad went to Melbourne and a few days later his dead body returned. His father had contracted meningitis and passed away at his sister-in-law's home in St Kilda. McEwen's life was turned upside down.

Though McEwen only spent his first seven years in Chiltern, and though his recollections of the town must have been tinged with great sorrow, early childhood memories were seared into him and he felt deeply connected to his birthplace all his life. McEwen felt such a great affinity for his hometown, that he had his career awards and honours housed not in the National Archives or the State Library but forwarded to the Chiltern Historical Society. Today, these are still on display at the unostentatious Chiltern Athenaeum Museum. There, in a single glass cabinet are photographs of McEwen laughing with US President Lyndon Bain Johnson alongside important diplomatic dossiers that he had kept, as well as his First Class Order of the Rising Sun (Kyokujitsu-Sho) which is among Japan's highest civil honours.

That a young man, a Chiltern local, who had reached the zenith of political life and sent evidence back to inspire others tells us that Place was clearly important to Jack.

For McEwen where you came from mattered, it shaped you and equally it should never constrain you.

Wangaratta

After becoming orphaned McEwen went to live with his maternal grandmother in Wangaratta, a regional town, 30km away. His grandmother Nellie Porter was running a boarding house there, after having sold the Royal Victoria Hotel on Faithful Street, from which you can still get a pot today. Nellie was a significant influence on McEwen's life, and was described by him later as a woman of 'considerable character' who encouraged him to be the very best he could.

McEwen's future political partner, Robert Menzies came from similar humble beginnings in tiny Jeparit in the Wimmera, western Victoria. But whereas Menzies went on to prestigious academic achievement, there were no Wesley College or Melbourne University colours on this future deputy prime minister's CV.

Attending the local State school, McEwen received his first merit certificate for academic achievement at age 12, but it would be the last as he would leave school the following year to work to contribute to the family budget. Born without wealth or privilege, McEwen's success came from an addiction to hard work, extraordinary self-belief, lived experience combined with a clear calling that centred in bettering the lot of rural Australians and therefore the nation.

Significantly, during this period, McEwen was raised in an all-female household made up of his sister, his aunts, his cousin and his grandmother. These were not easy times but *"despite being poor I had a happy childhood"*,[51] McEwen recalled. Being a smart young boy in an all-female household, the orphaned Jack would have almost certainly been the centre of attention, and the sole object of aspiration and expectations of his female relatives. Being favoured stood him in good stead in making him confident and in command, and in being able to take on many of the challenges he later encountered.

In his memoirs, McEwen recalls a striking piece of advice his grandmother used to give him and that it "moulded his outlook on life":

> *If you are going into the Church then become an Archbishop. If you go into the Army, become a General, if you go into politics, become the Prime Minister.*[52]

This is quite an astonishing precept from the matriarch of an impoverished Wangaratta family, especially considering Australia had only had four prime ministers at that point in history. Nellie passed away nine years prior to Jack becoming a member of parliament, but her impact on the man he became is incontrovertible.

For a widowed small businesswoman, caring for grandchildren and her own daughter, Nellie was a woman of strong opinion, whose resilience in the face of adversity is striking. Think for a moment the social status of this woman, her circumstances, away from the capital in Melbourne, and the heavy expectation she wove into young Jack. Nellie's aspiration for her grandson reflected the attitudes of a new young egalitarian nation, which was ahead of the world in enfranchisement in so many respects, and whose promise would not be limited by geography or social status.

In 1908, women had gained the right to vote in Victoria, but it would not be until 1923 that they had the right to stand for parliament. The Country Party had not yet been formed, but it was a time for heated political discussions about protectionism and free trade and labor laws across a nation not yet a decade old.

Around 1913, the extended family with Jack in tow had moved to Dandenong, then still a country town on the outskirts of Melbourne. Jack's first job was at a druggist's store in Melbourne's CBD that cemented the habit of the long work hours he was later renowned for in Canberra, catching the 6:30am train to Melbourne city and arriving back home after 7pm. The teenage McEwen, was independent and responsible even then, assisting his grandmother with the task of providing for the household, whilst carving out a brighter future. McEwen recalls that he was *"very conscious of the fact that my lack of education was not good enough,"* and *"I was determined to improve myself"*.[53]

Recognising that his ambitions would not be realised without self-improvement the young Jack studied after work, enjoying mathematics and geography but especially history. McEwen became incredibly well read despite his lack of formal education, possessing a clear mind and an ability to analyse. He successfully passed the entrance exam for the Commonwealth Public Service. His first position was working in the Solicitor General's office, where his clear mind and analytical capacity were recognised by, as circumstances had it, Gough Whitlam's father Fred who tried to unsuccessfully encourage him into law.

By the time Jack turned 16 he chose neither the church nor politics. Instead, he chose the army, doing his best to enlist before World War One ended like so many other young men. He again studied hard, gaining entry to Duntroon military college. He was determined to serve his nation in a practical way and so he rejected his grandmother's advice to "be a general" and upon turning 18 he signed up in the Australian Imperial Forces (AIF) which meant a quicker pathway to joining his fellow Australians overseas. However, the war ended just as he was ready for deployment. McEwen recalled that the rigours and hierarchy of the Army taught young Jack one thing - that he forever wanted to be 'free of a boss'. Instead he would determine his own future, eventually becoming the ultimate boss.

Stanhope

Despite the opportunities available to him in Melbourne, McEwen decided to return to his roots in country Victoria and began to be politically active in his local community. The Victorian Government's Rural Settlement Scheme or 'soldier settlements' gave McEwen his opportunity to be the master of his own destiny. The scheme repatriated soldiers who had served during the Great War, allocating a plot of undeveloped land and a capital grant to make improvements. After working across regional Victoria to gain experience in farming, McEwen selected a larger than average block and then worked extremely hard as a sole operator to develop the land. As he had little cash, off his own initiative he first took up work on the wharves as a volunteer unionist assuming a mate's name, to raise the capital needed to develop his farm. This formative period on the wharves was McEwen's first lesson in politics, teaching him a great deal about living with men who had conflicting views yet had to work side-by-side through rival unions.

Despite having no background in farming, through a combination of hard work, frugality, an eye for a good deal, and some luck, McEwen succeeded where the attrition rate was so high for other soldier-settlers.

The first years of farming involved dawn till dusk lonely, hard physical labour. Yet perhaps as a result of being parentless, McEwen recalled that: *"Loneliness, working on your block all day, never troubled me"*.[54] McEwen rarely if ever went to local dances, the pub, the races or the football - but instead chose to spend any precious free time on the farm reading history books at night by kerosene lamp. Even at 19 Jack was known to be thrifty and entrepreneurial, raising extra money by contracting out his pair of horses and by eating only the rabbits he trapped on his farm for over a year. This did, however, lead to a lifelong aversion to *lapin á la cocotte*.

In 1921, Jack married Annie McLeod who was from a farming family in Tongala. She was educated at prestigious Girton Girls Grammar boarding school in Bendigo but as a 'country girl' she worked side by side with young Jack to build a farm they could both be proud of. Selling the original 86 acre block, together they built their holding near Stanhope to in excess of 3,000 acres over the next four decades. Their property was appropriately named *Chilgala* (Chiltern-Tongala) an amalgam of his bride's place of birth and his. It was a place of joy, restorative hard work and tremendous pride for Jack throughout his career as an MP. He would spend weekends away from Canberra developing his farm, installing the latest agriculture technologies and systems. His interest in the farm never waned, and years later he would be on the phone daily from overseas trade missions or Canberra cabinet meetings seeking updates from his manager on stock prices, weather and water issues. Without an electorate office, constituents would also attend the farm to raise any concerns with their local Country Party MP.

Aside from a successful farming enterprise, Jack and Annie's marriage was also a politically profitable partnership. McEwen's new bride took what was most probably the unsolicited advice of Jack's ambitious grandmother Nellie, that it was her job to *"see him through his ambition - politics"* as Nellie had *"seen him through his three sacraments"*.[55] Nellie had proffered this more than a decade before Jack entered parliament. It was a task young Annie took seriously. Driving with Jack throughout his electorate so he could sleep or write speeches, hosting events, leading charity works, organising and speaking at Country Party or Country Women's Association (CWA) events and keeping a home fit for a deputy Prime Minister. Her work as the wife of an MP continued until severe illness stopped her, leading to a long time incapacitated, and she passed away in 1967.

All rural people must endure the struggles of drought, the elements, erratic commodity prices and marketing board issues, so finding time for thanksgiving is also woven into the seasons of their lives. In Stanhope their local celebration was *Mardi Gras*,[56] an annual street parade complete with floats, but held every New Year's Day eve. Even as Deputy Prime Minister Jack would stand on the back of a Bedford truck and officially open the event, enjoying this celebration of his small town. Both Jack and Annie were heavily involved in the community, including Lady McEwen hosting an annual garden party at *Chilgala*, whose gardens were renowned. Jack was also very much part of his local community as an active member of his Masonic Lodge.

There are a few in the district who remember Jack as a local, and both the farmer and the Deputy Prime Minister. Nationals stalwart and neighbor Frank Stevens recalls McEwen being chauffeured not only around the district, but also on more than one occasion on his farm in his big black Buick. The Buick (note not a protected Australian-made car) was a local legend having been seized by customs and procured by McEwen as his much loved government issued vehicle. McEwen held onto it because he loved the oversized (and fast) American cars. Frank, 40 years McEwen's junior, remembers being picked up from the front paddock of his farm by McEwen in order to settle a bet over some new Charolais calves. McEwen had earlier boasted to Frank that his inseminated calves would be a beautiful all-white progeny, while Frank, a pioneer in Charolais genetics, had wagered a bottle of whiskey that he would not get a solitary white calf. In trying to prove his point McEwen's chauffeur got "bogged to the axles" in one of the wet back paddocks at *Chilgala*. Frank remembers that the still suited McEwen splattered in mud from head to toe trying to get the Buick out of the bog; the McEwen-bred Charolais calves turned out to be salmon rather than white, but Frank never did get his bottle of whiskey.[57]

Local Stanhope farmer Murray Buzza also recalls but as a young child, McEwen calling around to visit his Dad on the neighbouring farm and McEwen sharing a story from Canberra: *"Billy Hughes known for his loud plaid suits was also hard of hearing. Thinking the former PM wouldn't hear him, Artie Fadden said to Jack, who was a young Minister as Hughes came in in a loud looking suit, 'that looks like the rug that Phar Lap died in!' And Billy Hughes said, 'I heard ya Fadden, I heard ya'".*[58]

Whilst 'Black Jack' was well known around the district, in the days before 24/7 media there were many electors who didn't even know what their MP looked like. When Jack presented at emergency room of the Rushworth hospital to be treated for his dermatitis he was not recognised. The exchange is purported to go something like this: "I am Jack McEwen, deputy prime minister" and "Yes, and I am the Queen of England" the local nurse replied. There was never a chance that Jack would 'get tickets' on himself with local feedback like that.

These stories (apart from the McEwen eccentricities) exemplify the total intertwining of the life of a Country Party member of Parliament. As B.D. Graham posits in his history of the formation of Australia's Country parties, the local regional MP was expected to be still grounded in his local community. Whilst he was not only required to deliver hard results in the form of roads, bridges and trade outcomes he was also expected to live as an *"honest countryman down to the last gesture"* proving he had not become corrupted by the city-bred politicians or persuaded to forsake his principles or constituents for the trappings of office.[59]

At 19 McEwen had joined the Victorian Farmers Union (soon to become the Victorian Country Party) to advocate for local soldier settlers. The soldier settler experiment was plagued with problems from the beginning as many former soldiers, often totally unsuited, unprepared and undercapitalised for a farmer's life, walked off the land. McEwen remained especially haunted by one neighbour who was unable to afford to bury his child. Meetings were held across the district as soldier settler farmers agitated for a better deal. McEwen's ability to articulate key facts and arguments was noted and despite being a relatively young man compared to others involved in the farming lobby, he was asked to lead delegations to Parliament in Spring Street to convince the State Government of the plight of northern Victoria's soldier settlers and their families. The Victorian Government's capital grant for soldier settlers was raised from 640 pounds to 1,000 pounds as a result of McEwen's lobbying efforts. Reflecting that period many years later he wept on the struggles of neighbouring soldier settlers, the bad behaviour of banks, and the lack of government support to impacted families from this period. As Stanhope local Bob Holschiver recalls, *"He was in there looking after the soldier settlers because he was one of them"*.[60] These experiences explain why for this future Minister, ensuring Australians were employed and able to support their family, was a foundational outcome of his policy perspective — a fair go for all, was McEwen's worldview borne from his lived experiences in northern Victoria.

During one delegation to Melbourne, young Jack had his very first encounter with the then Victorian Attorney General, Robert Menzies, who later recalled that *"the great advocate of the delegation was a dark-haired eager looking young man called John McEwen ... I've reminded him of it many times since and said, 'You know, you were terrifying even when you were quite young'!"*[61] It was Menzies who was to give McEwen his famous moniker 'Black Jack' for his dark features and darker temperament. In private meetings in Canberra, Menzies would refer to McEwen as simply 'Le Noir' (The Black).

At just 21, the same year he got married, the milk price collapsed and in response Jack began to organise the Stanhope dairy farmers into a co-operative. Pulling farmers together in a collective approach delivered a higher return and saw the dairymen with more control of their product in this growing rural community. McEwen led a delegation to inform Kyabram Butter Factory that he and his fellow dairymen would stop supplying milk, unless it agreed to sell the tiny weatherboard cheese factory Stanhope to new co-operative. With a 25 pound ($50) stake in the new co-operative, McEwen had become its largest shareholder and its first chairman at 23 years of age. McEwen went into sheep and beef production shortly afterwards, but the tiny cheese factory grew, serving the local dairy industry and the main employer in the district. Amazingly, it still exists today incorporated into global dairy giant Fonterra's current holdings.

The Places McEwen lived in during his formative years were part of him as he progressed his political career and straddled the world stage. He never forgot where he came from and the people he actually represented.

Country Victoria shaped McEwen's politics beliefs but more importantly his political methods. The difference between McEwen's collective bargaining at the Kennedy Round in Geneva and in Stanhope agripolitics was of scale not kind. McEwen was a man of Place.

3

PARTY

"It's not the size of the dog in the fight; but the size of the fight in the dog."

- Attributed to Mark Twain

September 1934. Australia is still in the grips of the Great Depression. A nervous 34-year-old McEwen steps for the first time onto a steamy train station platform in Queanbeyan, a few miles out from Canberra. Joining McEwen on their own journeys to Parliament House are a host of other first time MPs. Among them is Robert Menzies who already knows 'Black Jack' from his time as Victorian Solicitor-General as that indomitable young man who would berate him about the plight of soldier settlers. Also in the class of 1934 is Archie Cameron from South Australia – he and McEwen would later become fierce rivals for the Country Party leadership; McEwen eventually won and Cameron abandoned the party in protest, killing it in South Australia in the process. Then there is John Curtin, making his political comeback after winning back his Fremantle seat following Labor's electoral wipeout in 1931. In taking country Victoria to Canberra, McEwen was bringing more than his suitcase as baggage, and a decade of aggressive Victorian Country Party agri-politics.

Origin of the Country Party

McEwen's chosen political party, the Country Party is Australia's only political party based on overcoming the inequity that is grounded in geography. Jack McEwen embodies the political party he led like few other politicians in Australian political history. As B.D. Graham argues, Australia's Country parties (state and federal) are unique in the world as bodies of political expression for agriculture and rural communities; their longevity is a result of their origins as genuine grassroots organisations.[62]

The great strength of the Australian Country parties was the local leadership capability developed over decades of trial and error in running local farmers clubs, agricultural shows, the confidence gained in the lay church, in running the local Masonic lodges, and the lessons learned from the early trade union movement, which was at the time not exclusively Labor. It was these leadership skills and grassroot structures that have ensured the Australian Country Party survived and thrived.

The Country parties also grew from a belief that agriculture was the backbone of the national economy and should be recognised as such by government. Farmers tended to think of class as both a particular commodity producer group and their specific regional community.⁶³ The different challenges faced by individual producer groups such as dairymen against price fixing and market controls, the wheat farmers being subject to unstable economic circumstances and international commodity market vagaries, and the graziers who fought regulation of meat prices and tariff increases; came together in the Country Party and were simultaneously deeply committed to regional development.

Importantly, the Country parties were not landed gentry, but particularly so in Victoria. Agrarianism overseas was seen as an ennobling vocation, a moral imperative, whereas in Australia it was also about the rugged pioneer, linked to a sense of alienation from the cities. In Australia, farmers lacked the status and financial security enjoyed in other countries, often being disparaged as unsophisticated 'yokels', 'hayseeds' or 'cockies' by those in the cities. Farmers felt exploited by city interests. This mutual distrust between city and rural peoples that has been exacerbated with the decline of family links, is a key component to the Country Party's survival as compared with overseas examples.⁶⁴

In terms of cultural values, historian Russell Ward also argues it was this Australian form of agrarianism that gave us our national legend and values (mateship, adaptability, self-sufficiency and a collectivist ethic). They were the pastoral workers, the bushman. And it was McEwen's Country Party that saw itself as always about looking after the battler, whether they were an impoverished soldier settler family, a rural worker, or a small dairy farmer being exploited by the milk processor.

The Victorian Country Party

The history of the Country Party in Victoria is extremely complex and at times contradictory; personal rivalries stretch over decades, while the remnants of past schisms still exist today. From its formation during the World War One, there were two distinct constituencies in the Victorian Country Party, that made it quite different from other divisions. On one side there were the big established graziers, (the squatters from Banjo Patterson poems); they were traditionalists, liberal conservatives and free traders, who favoured forming coalitions with like-minded city folk. On the other side were the horticulturalists, vegetable and potato farmers, soldier settlers, dairymen, displaced miners and the like; they were unionists, sometimes radicals and fierce protectionists. As former leader of the Victorian Nationals Pat McNamara explains, the Victorian party was less western district and moleskins more *"overalls and grease, wheat cockies, dairy farmers and gumboots covered in cow shit"*.[65]

The soldier settlers were often the displaced children of Labor voters, denominationally diverse, inclined to favour a collective bargaining methodology, and practiced in solidarity. It was this group that originally formed the Victorian Farmers Union that would become the Victorian Country Party. As Peter Golding wrote, they called it a "union" because it was one. Historian B.D. Graham wrote in 1966:

> *Protectionism and free trade in rural Victoria, marked the difference between developed and under-developed regions. The economic confidence of the pastoral west was expressed in their belief in the open market. On the other hand, the insecurity of the new regions, the*

> Wimmera, the Goulburn Valley, the north-east, and east Gippsland, dictated their interest in protection against imports of primary produce, in sustained expenditure of public works development and in the north on the irrigation program.[66]

In McEwen's youth, the radical wing largely controlled the party and asserted its creed that the role of the party, if it could not win government in its own right (it occasionally did), was on the cross-bench, controlling the balance of power. However, it went further than that. Many of the radical Victorian Country Party members felt greater ideological affinity with the Labor Party that their parents had voted for than with the various incarnations of the future Liberal Party which they associated with Melbourne Grammar types.

The Victorian Country Party state leader Albert Arthur Dunstan had struck a covert agreement with the Labor Party which would make him the Premier of Victoria. Dunstan's back-room agreement was not a true coalition, just a mutual understanding on confidence and supply. The Country-Labor alliance was an open secret but could not be widely celebrated lest Dunstan lost the support of the graziers completely; he could not be seen to be openly supporting socialism.[67] The Masonic Lodges were influential local institutions in Victorian country towns whose members mirrored the Country Party branch members. McEwen rose through the ranks of the radicals as himself, Presbyterian and a Freemason.

This was the complex political world that McEwen ventured into in first seeking and eventually winning pre-selection in the first half of the 1930s. McEwen's first unsuccessful foray was into state politics for the state seat of Waranga in 1932, as a radical. With his background it makes sense that he was not an absolute individualist, seeing the power of groups of people banding together as a collective. As previously mentioned, McEwen formed a dairy farm co-op with neighbouring soldier settlers, knowing that together they could negotiate better prices than as individuals. While McEwen lost his first bid to enter politics, he performed so well that he succeeded shortly after by winning preselection in the 1934 federal campaign in the seat of Echuca after the sitting member resigned over the Country Party's Central Council making MPs sign the 'pledge'. The 'pledge' included directives to not enter into coalition agreements without the backing of the State lay party (people power); not to vote against the majority of the party caucus (solidarity) and to stand down if not endorsed party candidate (party first). Because McEwen was a part of the radical faction, the federal leader Dr Earle Page ran a candidate against him in this election. This early radicalism is an important part of the portrait of McEwen. McEwen, a hero of Australian conservatism, cut his teeth effectively as a union man.

Before McEwen's unsuccessful state parliament run, he had signed the Victorian division's 'Pledge'. However, when he arrived in Canberra, it quickly became clear to him that to have policy influence in Canberra, the Country Party needed to wield executive power. And so, he accepted a position in the Lyons United Australia Party (UAP) Cabinet in November 1937, therefore effectively declaring war with a large section of his own party at home in Victoria. The 'Pledge' highlighted the ownership the Victorian membership expected from their MPs. They were tired of sending good local men to Melbourne or Canberra for them to become gentrified and forget where they came from and who had sent them there. The Victorian Country Party expected their MPs to remember where their bread was buttered ... literally.

The all-powerful Victorian Country Party's Central Council expelled their newly minted minister McEwen in December 1937 for 'disloyalty,' for breaching 'the Pledge' and accepting a commission as a Lyons Government Minister for the Interior. This decision was to be ratified at the annual state conference in Ballarat. Perhaps, Premier Dunstan and Party President Hocking (who McEwen calls a "dictator") thought that McEwen would have no choice but to join the UAP or run as an independent at the next election; he could then be unseated and replaced with someone more compliant. Cross the party, lose your seat, good-bye McEwen.

However, they underestimated the man and his deep connection to the Country Party's membership. McEwen's 400-odd supporters walked out of Country Party State Conference. Explosively, the next day McEwen and his supporters held a rival meeting and formed a new party, the Liberal-Country Party. This was the second schism in the party in the previous 20 years. Importantly, the Liberal-Country Party kept McEwen a part of the Federal Country Party in Canberra until the schism in Victoria was repaired. McEwen had at least one member for every two Dunstan had - he had taken over a third of the party and barely even tried.

Decades later, these same tensions between the Victorian division and federal Country Party ministers flared up again at the State conference in Warrnambool. This time, the leader of the Victorian Parliamentary team was George Moss who reportedly had drunk in every pub in Victoria at least once. Moss continued to prosecute the separatist tradition of Dunstan aided and abetted by the State President Bruce Evans. As Nixon recalls:

> *Bruce Evans had cooked up this resolution and it had a lot of support and I said to Jack McEwen the day before in Canberra, 'Jack, you'll have to come. They'll chew me up and spit me out, these folks. So you'll have to come. I said, no damn fair. You're going to come.' So we flew down. Bruce Evans got up and moved this resolution and McEwen, got to his feet. And he absolutely slammed them. He said to Bruce Evans, 'Now tell me Mr Evans, what resolutions have you had carried and passed as legislation in the parliament?' And he said, 'of course the answer is none. And you never will have.' Jack said, he got his name on the statute books, the legislation that he brought in and he'd have it there a dozen times, 20 times, a hundred times. But you can't do that sitting in the corner here. You're a nothing, you're a nothing.*[68]

This deeply entrenched ideological and cultural divide within the rank and file membership of Victoria still echoes today. Following Jeff Kennett's disastrous election result in 1999, where three regional seats were lost to rural independents and the safe seat of Benalla was lost to Labor at the 2000 by election when Nationals Leader Pat McNamara resigned, the Nationals (the modern Country Party formally and dramatically broke the coalition with the Victorian Liberal Party under the leadership of Peter Ryan. It is important to understand this divide within the Victorian Country Party.

McEwen's ability to straddle the Country Party's internal tensions — between individualism and interdependence, between free trade and protection, speaks to his extraordinary political acumen. As Golding says, *"He was a political gladiator, each foot on the saddle of a different charger both fighting for the lead and only his persuasive strength on the reins keeping them from diverging"*.[69] The only way to achieve outcomes with this sort of internal tension is by approaching it pragmatically and realistically. He faced down many internal divisions throughout his career by explaining the practical, real life impact of any given proposal he didn't agree with.

There are obvious parallels between the grassroots Victorian Country Party and its political wing and the Australian Labor Party. The Labor Party executives' dominance and demand for uniformity has many times led to schisms in their Party, and it is not surprising that the same demands led to the same outcomes for the Country Party. The experience had a lasting effect on McEwen. As he mused about Labor:

> *Labor leaders, and Labor members generally, are under great pressure to toe the party line, because the rules of the game make the party machine supreme. I will always maintain that a Labor leader who says 'Whatever the party decides is my policy' is giving evidence of a weakness that can be exploited. What you get is the uninformed dictating to the informed. You get the executive of the party organization dictating to ministers...*[70]

McEwen was not led exclusively by personal ambition. The tensions outlined are replicated within the man himself. He later had the chance to be prime minister but turned it down because it would mean leaving the Country Party which he described as 'unthinkable'. McEwen was led by his belief that to actually influence policy in Canberra on issues he and his party cared about, like addressing unemployment and finding new export markets for farmers, the Country Party needed a strong and permanent presence in cabinet. As Bruce Lloyd, his successor in the seat of Murray said, *"the biggest things with McEwen in my view was that the Country Party could not be ignored on anything and that through McEwen his own presence was dominant enough to ensure that"*.[71]

The Country Party in Canberra

The federal politics of the 1930s, when McEwen arrived on the scene, was, compared with Victoria, almost as chaotic. Within the chaos, the Country Party could only eek out occasional influence on the statute book. There are similarities between the 1930s Country Party with the Australian Democrats in the 1990s Senate, fighting with other minor parties for the trinkets of government.

The landscape McEwen and his colleagues stepped off the train and onto the platform for their first sitting week was completely different to today. Geographically, Canberra six years after becoming the nation's capital, consisted of just a few large public buildings and only 7,000 residents. Politically, it was a wild west, though a cordial and well-mannered one. There were only 74 MPs and 36 senators, and they were all men in those days. Politicians of all stripes lived together, drank together and played billiards together in the Canberra and the Kurrajong hotels. Despite often being friends, the politicians of this era were just as ambitious as their modern counterparts and their machinations were as guileful, but their politics more fluid, and the ideological boundaries of the parties more porous. Having survived the chaos of the Victorian division of the Country Party to finally arrive in Canberra as an MP, McEwen was about to walk into a period of Australian politics of now long-forgotten camaraderie but equally a period of fluidity and political bastardry within and between political parties.

Nothing exemplifies the shifting partisan sands of McEwen's first years in Canberra than the intrigue leading up to the 1934 Melbourne Cup. After the election in which McEwen first entered the Parliament, the UAP had lost its absolute majority. Almost concurrent with Dunstan's machinations in Melbourne, the new arithmetic on the house floor left Prime Minister Lyons in a precarious position – he could whip only 33 members, Scullin Labor 18 MPs, Page 14 for the Country Party and John Beasley had 9 members for Lang Labor, the independent NSW Labor faction. Lyons made a half-hearted offer to Page to try to create a majority coalition, but Page felt that Lyons' offer still gave the Country Party insufficient representation in cabinet to the extent that Page saw it as sacrificing his party's independence.

The 1934 Melbourne Cup was to be extra special because it was 100 years since the establishment of the colony of Victoria. As part of the celebrations, Prince Henry, the Duke of Gloucester, was sailing from England to attend. It was therefore expected that all the ministers and federal Victorian parliamentarians were likewise to attend this auspicious occasion. When Prime Minister Lyons moved what he thought was a routine motion to adjourn Parliament for an extra day so that members could go to next week's Cup, he was oblivious to a plot that had been hatching in the backstalls of Parliament House. The 'Race that Stops a Nation', was about to stop a government.

As Lyons sat down, Page stood up at his cross bench in a simulated rage. The Country Party, he said, would not vote for the Prime Minister's motion. Lyons was likely taken aback and confused at this unexpected turn of events. Next, Jack Beasley stood up. New MP McEwen watched in shock as Beasley said that Lang's Labor agreed wholeheartedly with Page and that the Prime Minister's motion was a disgrace.

Page and Beasley had, of course, pre-arranged this charade in secret. The genius of their collusion was that because the Country Party, and worse, Lang Labor, had stolen the mantle of 'opposition' from the Labor Opposition, Scullin was also put in an awkward position. This, of course, was Beasley's aim and why he decided to partake in the plan. There was only one thing Scullin could do to save face. And so, the Opposition Leader also condemned the Prime Minister's motion and said that Labor was not going to support it either. Extraordinarily, the three non-government parties were going to out-vote the minority government on what was supposed to be the most innocent of motions.

As the debate raged around him, a stunned Lyons was left sitting on his bench contemplating this humiliating situation — he was a prime minister who could not even adjourn Parliament, and with Prince Henry's ship bearing down on Port Phillip, Lyons and his Ministers would be unable to greet him lest a quorum started passing legislation in Canberra in their absence.

These events were highly formative for McEwen and a

lesson in the effective application of political pressure that would later be instructive in his famous stand-off against Billy McMahon in the 1960s. As McEwen recalls:

> *This was a stunning situation, foreseen only by Page and Beasely. Debate on the motion, as I remember it, went on for a very long time while people thought through the consequences of what was happening. Frank Brennan, a Labor member of the day, later recounted the peregrinations of the various party emissaries running on the floor of the House and through the basement corridors of Parliament while the debate was going on and they were trying to fix up what really could be done. We succeeded in getting an adjournment of the debate carried and went on to other business. Lyons sent for Page and practically said, "Well Doc, what's your price?"*[72]

The Grafton medico Dr Page's demands were the *de facto* deputy prime ministership, the commerce portfolio for himself, plus one more ministerial position and two additional assistant ministers for the Country Party. Despite his inexperience, McEwen would assume one of those ministerial positions three years later when Lyons made him his Minister for the Interior. The later tradition of the National Party leader being Deputy Prime Minister in a coalition government stems from this Melbourne Cup stand-off.

Country Party in Coalition

McEwen was Country Party through and through. McEwen fought his whole life for the strength of an independent

Country Party, knowing it was the only avenue to secure the fortunes of regional Australia. However, McEwen was also a pragmatist. He believed that he could be most effective in achieving his goals and fighting for regional Australia by wielding the power and authority of a cabinet minister. Only as Agriculture Minister could McEwen have protected the Australian wool clip when America sought to 'compulsorily acquire' it during the Korean War; only as Minister for Trade could he have opened up new export markets in Asia and America for Australian primary industry. Yet McEwen never allowed the Country Party to become the deferential member of the Coalition. In 13 years of party leadership, McEwen only twice threatened the Liberals with the breakup of the Coalition. One of the 'red-lines' was electoral redistribution, the other (channelling Page regarding Menzies) was over his hated rival Billy McMahon becoming PM, although on this he eventually relented a few years later as he retired.

Paul Kelly's assessment of the Country Party during this period is especially informative, he argues they were not ideologues driven to implement a textbook neoclassical economic theory. Rather, they were men of action, joining the dots of a society to build economic strength.[73] Deep pragmatism born of Place, where people live and work, succeeding or failing with the seasons, understanding the need to work with natural organic systems rather than struggling to harness them. The Country Party is as much the practice of politics as a philosophy.

One of McEwen's most significant legacies to Australian politics is his pivotal role in developing and maintaining the stable, successful and formidable partnership between the independent Liberal and National parties. He also ensured the oversized strength of the Country Party's position within that partnership to deliver for regional Australia. This powerful Coalition is now taken for granted by some, considered the default arrangement in Australian conservatism, but as shown, it was not always this way, nor is it set in stone even now. It was McEwen and the successors that he mentored, Peter Nixon, Doug Anthony and Ian Sinclair, who demonstrated to both parties what could be achieved through the partnership of these two independent parties. In McEwen's words "*there has always been a section of the Liberal Party who wished the Country Party would disappear*". But McEwen, especially in partnership with Menzies, was able to navigate the complexities of separate and sovereign parties and political traditions. Together, governing as one in the national interest, they could focus on "*the survival of the country and the uplifting of living standards*".[74]

When McEwen first took his seat in the Commonwealth Parliament, there was no such thing as 'The Coalition'. The two major conservative parties of the day were his Country Party and the United Australia Party. They were deeply distrustful of each other. A conservative coalition would only ever be proposed if there was no other way for the non-Labor forces to form government, and unlike today, it would never be secure.

McEwen was so effective at being a minister that Menzies and his new Liberal Party slowly came to view partnership with the Country Party not as an occasional necessary inconvenience, but as beneficial for good governance in the national interest. Some credit for this needs to go to Page and Fadden. Credit also needs to go to Nixon, Anthony and Sinclair whose sheer competence allowed McEwen's gains for the Country Party to be maintained through the Fraser era and onwards. The Country Party reflected the regional communities it represented, resilient, independent yet communal. McEwen was of the Country Party. He embodied the Party.

The Coalition governments of the post-World War Two era are now looked back on as the halcyon days of Australian conservatism. And with all due respect to Artie Fadden who had his own virtues, it was the political partnership of McEwen and Menzies that forged the durability of a broader coalition that has underpinned stable federal governments for 50 out of the 75 years following the World War Two. All subsequent federal coalition governments are in some sense modelled on the political union of Menzies and McEwen. Both Malcolm Fraser and John Howard had opportunities to keep the Nationals off the government benches if they had wanted, excluding Ian Sinclair and Tim Fischer respectively. Both, in their wisdom, chose to keep the Coalition together, in part, to recapture some of the magic of that devastating combination of Menzies and McEwen — the urbane but aloof philosopher and the austere straightforward pragmatist, patriots both. As McEwen summed up his commitment to the Country Party towards the end of his political career:

> *I have great devotion to my Party. I am tremendously proud of it and tremendously indebted to it. I have said before that all the opportunities I had arose because the Country Party allowed me to carry its brand. It was as a representative of the Country Party that I stood*

for Parliament, that I went into the Cabinet, that I am Deputy Prime Minister, and I am never unconscious of the fact that the Country Party is the basis of all that I am and have been. [75]

Molnar, George. ([195-?]). "Oh well! Then we'll strike again." Retrieved November 27, 2020, from http://nla.gov.au/nla.obj-147569318

Molnar, George. (1955). "On second thought that includes you too." Retrieved November 27, 2020, from http://nla.gov.au/nla.obj-147532903

4

PATRIOT

"Men love their country not because it is great, but because it is their own."

- Seneca

McEwen was truly Australian in a way that many of the country's other contemporaneous leaders were not, particularly on the conservative side of politics. Consider Prime Minister Stanley Bruce (1923-1929), or Viscount Bruce of Melbourne as he was known once he attained peerage. Bruce was Australia's High Commissioner to the UK during McEwen's early career and is said to have once remarked that his most prized possessions were his membership of the Royal Society, his Cambridge Blue in rowing and his captaincy of St Andrew's Royal and Ancient Golf Club![76] Richard Casey was Lyons' Treasurer, later Menzies' Ambassador to the

US, and then the Governor-General, and while McEwen described him as "nationally-minded" Casey chose to spend the last years of his life as Baron Casey of Berwick (of the Gippsland variety) in the House of Lords. Then there was Menzies. To be fair, Menzies was patriotic in his own way, but most historians agree that first and foremost he was an Empire man. McEwen was different. He did not think about Australia as a mere dominion of the Empire in the way that Bruce, Casey, Menzies and frankly most conservatives tended to at this time. McEwen was highly ambitious, but he was of another ilk. McEwen did not spend his 20s drinking port in any fancy Oxbridge dining hall, he spent them mostly in solitude on his 86 acre soldier-settler block in the Goulburn Valley, living off the rabbits he shot and teaching himself how to be a dairy farmer. His public life was always about promoting the national well-being - for McEwen it was always Australia First.

'Black Jack' McEwen just loved Australia. As a teenager, McEwen was desperate to serve his country in the First World War in any way he could, and his deep love never waned throughout his life. Robert Macklin, his press secretary from 1967 until his retirement, recalled McEwen speaking frequently about *"this great treasure that is Australia"*.[77] McEwen often judged the character of other men by their patriotism. For example, of Billy Hughes, McEwen said *"(he) had what I respect above all things — a tremendous feeling for his country"*.[78] Of John Curtin, McEwen praised his ability to *"take on the people in his own party when he felt that the well-being of Australia required it,"* calling him a *"very great man"*.[79] Politically, McEwen expressed his love of country by making decisions through the prism of 'the national interest'.

The Patriot fights for sovereignty

None of this is to say that McEwen was anti-Britain or anti-monarchy in any way; it is exactly the opposite. In his memoirs, McEwen recalls with derision the anti-British feeling he believed was rife in the Labor Party that drew so much Irish Catholic support, highlighting with consternation, for example, longtime Labor MP Frank Brennan calling the British navy *"the most evil thing in the world"*[80] in a speech in the House. McEwen thought Australia was lucky that a strong-willed man like John Curtin happened to be leader of the Labor Party during World War Two, speculating that many other Labor members might not have had the appetite to fight fascism under the Union Jack.

Yet the almost reverent anglophilia prevalent on the conservative benches brought its own problems. It was this dutiful deference to the mother country that had left Australia with such a bad trade deal with its coloniser, the Ottawa Agreement. Britain was at the time our biggest trading partner, but the Ottawa Agreement had been struck in desperation during the Great Depression, and while it might have served the country adequately in its early years, McEwen thought Australia was increasingly being fleeced. McEwen set about rectifying the situation when he became Minister for Trade in the second Menzies Government. In 1956, together Menzies and McEwen left Australia for Britain to secure a better deal for the nation. It says something about the difference in the temperaments of Menzies and McEwen that Prime Minister Menzies chose a leisurely journey to London aboard his ship the *Arcadia*, while McEwen, the no-nonsense pragmatist, flew. Ever the work horse, McEwen made stop-offs in countries along the way to make various trade and diplomacy inquiries. Whilst Menzies was deployed to negotiate for Britain in the Suez crisis, McEwen was focused on the original purpose of their trip. He was determined not to leave London without a new trade deal for Australia. The plight of Australian farming communities was always front of mind even in corridors of Whitehall and Westminster.

The British negotiators were not used to dealing with Australian representatives with McEwen's single-mindedness. He took them by complete surprise with his perseverance and frankness. McEwen was joined at the negotiation table by his right-hand man, John Crawford. McEwen had hand-picked Crawford as his Secretary of Trade and Industry, and in trade philosophy they were of the same mind. Crawford later reflected that *"a distinct improvement in the level of performance of the UK ministerial team in 1956 occurred after they realised the quality of the Australian minister"*.[81] McEwen and Crawford had come to London with an extremely difficult set of objectives: get Britain to reduce tariffs on Australian exports as much as possible, to commit to purchasing Australian wheat, to agree to Australia rescinding its preference for importing British manufactured goods, and to accept Australia having greater flexibility in pursuing other markets. In short, McEwen and Crawford sought to comprehensively restructure the trading relationship. Fairer, more flexible, freer trade. The British were not particularly keen on any of these propositions. At one point, McEwen recalled his British counterparts telling him that English millers and bakers did not find Australian wheat acceptable for their bread and that only English or Canadian wheat would do.

Perhaps a Menzies or a Bruce would 'culturally cringe' at this point. Not McEwen. He simply replied, *"we seem to be able to bake bread in Australia"*.[82] The British did not pursue that line of argument further.

Nevertheless, the British continued to be intransigent for five weeks of protracted negotiations. Eventually, McEwen had to be blunt: *"I said ... that before I left Australia, Cabinet decided we would sooner have no trade treaty at all than have one as unbalanced as the existing arrangements."*[83] In other words, McEwen told the British that no deal is better than a bad deal! McEwen and Crawford had to make an additional trip to London six weeks later, but eventually they secured a new trade deal achieving much of what they set out to do. Unfortunately, it was not as good a deal as it could have been, as according to Crawford *"were it not for the intervention of Prime Minister Menzies, the terms of the new trade agreement ... would (and quite fairly) have been tougher for the United Kingdom than in fact they were. Specifically, the margin of tariff preference granted on imported from the UK would have been less than that finally accepted by McEwen"*.[84] Nevertheless, it was McEwen's first big win as a Trade Minister and proved to be one of his greatest — a massive boon for Australian primary industry, particularly for the wheat growers, whose wheat, it seems, English bakers found acceptable after all.

The Patriot takes on vested interests

In April of 1939, Prime Minister Lyons died of a heart attack and Menzies was seen as the most logical successor in the UAP. However, Page hated Menzies on a personal level and, with the help of Archie Cameron, launched a serious personal attack on him on the floor of Parliament. Lyons' coalition was broken and the Country Party itself was of two minds. In part, this was driven by the issue of wheat prices. The wheat price was causing the Country Party instability, as wheat farmers were subjected to variability of international markets and unfavourable seasonal conditions.

In August 1939 (bear in mind the date), the same people who sought to expel McEwen from the Victorian Country Party convened a meeting on the wheat crisis, at the newly finished art deco Numurkah Town Hall. Numurkah was the largest wheat town in McEwen's electorate, the hall was packed over 500 local farmers crowded in to give their MP a piece of their mind. Menzies' UAP was against the Country Party position of a guaranteed wheat price pegged to the domestic economy. Irate farmers shouted for a better deal from the federal government and expected their man, Jack McEwen MP, to back his party and his people. The debate was vocal and strident, culminating in a demand for McEwen to end the Coalition in support of his local farmers, his wheat towns. He stared his opponents down. Jack reminded them that Australia could be at war at any time over the coming weeks and McEwen, ever the patriot, refused to have Australia in a general election, politically unstable entering a war. As McEwen tells it, half the room cheered, the other half booed.

At the time, Menzies was leading a minority federal government, and Page saw this issue as his opportunity to strike a fatal blow to his own mortal enemy. Jack may have convinced half of his growers in regional Victoria but meanwhile Page had convinced the rest of the Country Party divisions that the wheat price was a totemic issue. The

Country Party would be voting for wheat farmers with the Labor Party, and thus the federal government would fall: *"the fate of the government depended on its attitude to wheat"*.[85] Decision made, all that remained was for parliament to return and a vote be put to the floor. However, that same afternoon, local newspapers headlined "Hitler Bombs Warsaw". Within weeks Australia was at war, the wheat price and Page's revenge were forgotten.

On reflection McEwen said, *"there are a thousand interesting events in the sort of life I have lived, but this was one that not only affected my career but could also have affected the Australian nation"*. That the local need of his farmers, his Party and his nation were in tension was a rare occurrence for McEwen. Would he have crossed the floor? Against Page and his own patriotic principles? McEwen always fought for his party, even when that meant fighting against it. His sound judgement, in a hall of angry farmers was ultimately vindicated as the clouds of war descended. As McEwen said:

> *The stand I had taken at Numurkah was seen to be fully justified. It was unthinkable to now try and bring down the government. But if the meeting had been held a month earlier, our federal members would have been at great pressure to vote against the government and we would have been in the middle of a general election when the war was declared.* [86]

The Patriot makes hard decisions in the national interest

McEwen was a patriot, but more than that, he had a sense of confidence in the capability and potential of his country. He brought a spirit of national self-confidence to cabinets that often sorely needed it. On the other hand, Menzies' almost visceral anglophilia could sometimes be a weakness. It underpinned his wartime thinking far too much and this, in part, undid his first prime ministership.

In the lead up to the war, with tensions rising in both Europe and Asia, there was a growing realisation in Australia that the motherland was no longer capable of defending Australia. In 1939, feeling increasingly isolated from Britain, the Australian Government started making overtures to America. Yet, meetings that Menzies' people had with President Franklin D. Roosevelt's advisers indicated that Australia was the last thing on the mind of the United States.

Fearing that Australia might be forsaken by the mother country, she also could not rely on help from Uncle Sam. Our leaders were beginning to grapple with a hitherto inconceivable idea — Australia was alone in the world. In the midst of the learned helplessness of our leaders, there were some patriots who rose to meet the occasion — McEwen was one. McEwen, who never knew his mother and whose father died when he was seven, had been alone in the world his whole life. Perhaps this made McEwen psychologically better prepared than his colleagues to lead Australia through the self-reliance that the impending war would thrust upon the nation.

Recall that facing the prospect of war, McEwen had stared down his own party on wheat to back the stability of the existing Menzies minority government. However, it became McEwen's view that wartime Menzies had *"too great a sensitivity to the expenditure of large sums of money,"*[87] and this was endangering both the safety of the nation and the welfare of our troops. In August 1941, government ministers including McEwen, Earle Page, Harold Holt, and Billy Hughes knew that Menzies needed to be replaced as Prime Minister and they told him that he no longer had their support. After being elected at a government joint party room meeting, the Country Party's Artie Fadden was sworn in as Prime Minister of a minority government. He held the position for 40 days from 29 August to 7 October until Curtin, with the support of two independents initiated a vote of no confidence in the House and drove to Yarralumla.

The Patriots protects their nation in war

One of McEwen's greatest achievements and acts of patriotism, is also one of his least known. It is a quiet achievement that protected Australia from invasion. Historians and commentators have too often failed to bring attention to the handful of strategically pivotal decisions that were made during the Menzies-Fadden wartime government. Chief among these was a clandestine operation in New Caledonia jointly masterminded by John McEwen, the British High Commissioner in Fiji, and General Charles de Gaulle, the Free French leader. This little known operation was a bloodless *coup d'état* that was key in impeding the dreaded Japanese invasion of Australia in the years that followed. It is a story of intrigue and deceit that shows McEwen at his finest — scrupulous yet bold. It is not an overstatement to say that McEwen's ever-so-careful intervention may have saved Australia. Japanese on home soil was a very real possibility at that time.

In 1940, the war in Europe was going very badly and soon France fell under Nazi occupation. Hitler installed a puppet government, the Vichy regime. With Hitler controlling France, the French possessions in the Asia-Pacific, specifically New Caledonia and the New Hebrides, became security risks to the Australian mainland. In a worst-case scenario it was envisioned that the islands might be gifted to the Japanese and become military bases from which attacks could be launched. The capital of New Caledonia, Noumea is fewer than 1500 kms from Brisbane.

The Australian Military Chiefs advised that any preemptive Australian interference in New Caledonia could hasten a retaliatory Japanese invasion of the Netherlands East Indies (Indonesia). In the likely ensuing escalation, Australia would have no hope of holding the islands against Japanese sea power, and worse, could hasten a war with Japan that Menzies at this point still hoped could be avoided. At this time, Japan was an imperial force in Asia and while friendly with Hitler and Mussolini, Japan had not yet committed to an official alliance. Because of this, Britain and Australia both sought a statement from President Roosevelt expressing that the United States desired for the *status quo* to be preserved in the French Pacific. The US had not yet joined the Allies in the war.

On 18 June, the same day General de Gaulle began his famous resistance broadcasts on the BBC, the Australian War Cabinet sent a summary of its concerns to British Prime Minister Winston Churchill. The document reveals that the Australian War Cabinet had determined that there were two courses of action in New Caledonia and they sought British advice on which to follow:

1. That the USA might exercise the same deterrent effect as in the case of the Netherlands East Indies;

2. That we might take action to forestall Japan by occupation with our forces.[88]

The British reply arrived in Australia on 21 June. In essence it said: 'Please do nothing.' It explained that Britain was already asking President Roosevelt to issue a statement to deter Japan from taking the islands. This is unsurprising as the British Cabinet was, at the time, still reeling from the Dunkirk evacuation and some even favoured signing a deal with Hitler rather than fighting on.

The actual situation on the ground in New Caledonia was complex. Its Governor, a man called Georges Pélcier, was stuck between a rock and a hard place. Constitutionally, he would be answerable to the regime that Hitler was installing in France, but the people he governed were largely loyal to Free France and Charles de Gaulle. Complicating the matter, New Caledonia relied heavily on Australia for food supplies. Governor Pélcier committed to Menzies to continue the fight by the side of the British Empire and her allies, and in the same telegram requested additional Australian flour.[89] Following this telegram, much of the panic in Canberra subsided.

But 'Black Jack' McEwen was not convinced. According to his memoirs, the then Minister for the External Affairs (Foreign Minister) was worried and, perhaps even at this early stage, privately came to believe that the government of New Caledonia would need to be replaced for the sake of the safety of the Australian mainland.[90] However, McEwen was also wary of the implications of drastic action and knew he needed more information. McEwen decided he needed to go on a fact-finding mission. On 26 June, his Department handed McEwen a comprehensive memorandum informing him of the status of all French territories that could affect Australia including the Kerguelen Archipelago and the Islands of St Paul and Amsterdam in the South Indian Ocean, Adelie Land (France's Antarctic claim that intersected Australia's), Indochina, New Caledonia, and the New Hebrides Franco-British condominium.[91] The memorandum strongly urged McEwen against any Australian intervention probably because McEwen had already expressed his private view. The Department advised McEwen that merely preserving the *status quo* should be the extent of his and the Government's aim. McEwen agreed — for now.

On the same day as he received the memorandum, McEwen contacted Australia's Ambassador to the United States, Richard Casey asking him to express to the Roosevelt Administration that Australia also hoped for a US public declaration supporting the maintenance of the *status quo* in the French Pacific. It was in the strategic interests of the United States to do so as a hostile or Japanese-controlled New Caledonia would endanger trans-pacific air routes and worse, threaten American Samoa.

McEwen then decided that he needed his own man in Noumea to quietly keep close tabs on the situation and who would report directly to him on everything Governor Pélcier was doing.[92] McEwen contacted an Australian solicitor living in the New Hebrides called B.C. Ballard who was fluent in French, and well-versed in French political thinking — the perfect man for the job.[93] In early August, McEwen sent Ballard to Noumea to gather political and strategic information. McEwen had a spy.

The declassified mission briefing, states three telling instructions to Ballard explaining McEwen's plan: Ballard was to

- *"Make regular secret reports as to the attitude of the Governor, the Advisory Council, public officials and the general population towards the Vichy Government on the one hand and towards General de Gaulle... on the other.";*
- *"make reports to the Commonwealth Government upon all Japanese activities in New Caledonia.";* and
- *"To carry out such other functions as the Minister for External Affairs* (John McEwen) *shall from time to time direct."*[94]

There had been a further complication. On 3 August, Menzies received a MOST SECRET telegram from Australian high Commissioner Bruce in London. In a paragraph labeled SPECIALLY SECRET, Bruce disclosed that London had become aware that a Japanese agent called Tokitaro Kuroki had arrived in Noumea, New Caledonia. McEwen's spy now had a rival Japanese counterpart.

McEwen soon realised that the theory of maintaining the *status quo* made no sense. The idea of a New Caledonian Government that was constitutionally an arm of Hitler's Vichy regime but *de facto* fighting on the side of the Allies would be untenable. Australia did not yet know it, but McEwen was right. Governor Pélcier had been secretly acquiescing to the Vichy regime. New Caledonians who instead supported de

Gaulle were furious about it, demanding his resignation. One brave New Caledonian man called Raymond Pognon deserves individual recognition for forming a secret de Gaullist committee and making contact with General de Gaulle himself.

Nevertheless, it wasn't long before a sloop from Vichy France called the *Dumont d'Ourville* arrived. The captain of the sloop was a no-nonsense military type determined to follow orders and uphold the Vichy regime. He came with gendarmes and took control of the islands. All the while, McEwen was receiving regular reports from his spy. But Japan's man on the ground, Tokitaro Kuroki, was laying the groundwork for Emperor Hirohito. The situation was getting serious. Australia was in danger.

On 30 August, McEwen's spy delivered a top secret report:

> *Popular movement undoubtedly strong and opposed to Governor whom they suspect of playing a double game and of having brought sloop here to intimidate them,"* Ballard wrote, *"The Governor says the people do not know what making war means. Rumours are being spread, I think officially, that Australia desires to annex New Caledonia to the Commonwealth of Australia.*[95]

McEwen had a confidential one-on-one conversation with the Prime Minister at Parliament House. McEwen told Menzies that action needed to be taken or Australia risked a Japanese military base on its doorstep from which attacks or even a full-scale invasion of Australia could be launched. *"I said to Menzies, I think we ought to try to get control of New Caledonia by aggressive diplomacy."* Reportedly, Menzies replied *"All right. Have a go at it"*.[96] The plan was to replace the New Caledonian Governor with the current Governor of the New Hebrides, Sautot, who was pro-de Gaulle and so pro-Allies.⁹⁷

McEwen's operation had to be a total secret. It was not discussed in Cabinet as a leak to the press could not be risked lest it alert the Vichyists in Noumea. McEwen's memoirs hold that the only people in the Government who knew about it were Menzies and himself, but declassified documents show that some others including McEwen's rival for the Country Party leadership, *de facto* deputy PM Archie Cameron also knew about it in his capacity as Minister for the Navy, although he disapproved. The moment of truth had arrived and neither the riskiness of the plan, nor size of the stakes was not lost on anyone.

McEwen devised to put the Sautot on a chartered Norwegian cargo vessel to smuggle him into Noumea. McEwen then arranged for the *HMAS Adelaide*, an Australian cruiser, to in his words *"just so happen"* to put in at Noumea on the same day. When the two ships arrived in the bay, word of a *ralliement* for freedom spread through the city and into the New Caledonian bush. People flooded the streets of the capital singing the national anthem of Free France, *La Marseillaise*. With the streets packed full of French patriots, and an Australian cruiser in the bay that was more match for Hitler's French sloop, the Vichyists knew there was no way to resist. Over the subsequent days they submitted peacefully to Australia and the pro-de Gaulle governor, Sautot, was installed. The deposed officials were put on the same Norwegian cargo ship and dropped off near Saigon (Ho Chi Minh City). The operation could not have gone more peacefully or smoothly.

Sautot became the new New Caledonian Governor and would eventually prove a vital ally to both Australia and the United States through the war, allowing New Caledonia to become a US base rather than a Japanese one. Many New Caledonians would volunteer alongside American and Australian troops in the Pacific War. Their *ralliement*, or the 'one-man revolution' as de Gaulle reportedly once called it while reminiscing with McEwen during a 1962 trade negotiation,[98] proved to be a strategically pivotal moment in the Pacific War. Today, on a hill overlooking Noumea, a great bronze Cross of Lorraine, the symbol of Free France, stands in memory of the *ralliement* that McEwen made possible. McEwen believed that it was the most important thing he ever did.

Aristotle once said that courage is the mid-point between timidity and recklessness. By that definition, the decisions McEwen the Patriot made throughout this one month of his life demonstrate an epic courage in the man, neither carelessly rushing in nor shying away from the enormity of the stakes. As the French say *'de l'audace, encore de l'audace, toujours de l'audace.'* — courage, more courage, ever more courage.[99]

The Patriot has a vision for their nation

"What of the future? We Australians have so much running for us that I am confident we shall continue to grow and expand. Australia is one of the few countries in the world that is not only self-sufficient in food and important raw materials but has an export surplus in these things. We have a sophisticated workforce and a sophisticated field of management that enables us, in a highly

competitive world, to continue to grow as a manufacturing. It would be a great mistake if our manufacturing potential were to be neglected or underestimated. So, considering our self- sufficiency in food and materials, our capacity for industrial growth and our tremendous land area capable of absorbing additional population form around the world,I look forward with a high level of confidence to the future of Australia". [100]

[When he was Prime Minister after the death of Harold Holt, John McEwen asked Sir Charles Spry, the head of ASIO, for information about Maxwell Newton, a journalist associated with McEwen's political rival, Bill McMahon, and who was a publicist for the Japan External Trade Organisation (JETRO)] [picture] / O'Neill

McCrae, Stewart. (1968). "Don't worry John! I could always give it a blast with this!" [John McEwen holding a tough budget gun watching John Gorton chasing an inflation butterfly] Retrieved November 27, 2020, from http://nla.gov.au/nla.obj-145842733

5

POWER

"Let your plans be dark and impenetrable as night, and when you move, fall like a thunderbolt."

- Sun Tzu, The Art of War

McEwen understood power, the currency of politics. He knew how to bring people with him. He understood the power of the press and could control public narratives. He amassed knowledge, contacts and intelligence and surveilled his enemies. He demanded precise detail in briefs to make sure he was ready for any surprise attacks or opportunities. But his power was more than cerebral, or a full teledex, it was physical. Those who still remember McEwen associate him with one word, presence. Nixon says, "He had a real presence, an absolute real presence. He never walked anywhere, he strode. He'd walk into a room and wouldn't have even opened his mouth, but he'd dominate the room".[101]

Long time Canberra Press Gallery journalist Alan Reid's peerless prose sums up perfectly McEwen's relationship with power:

> *Self-made, self-contained but passionate, wealthy but austere, McEwen had the aloof dignity of a patrician, a Corsican-like devotion to the pursuit of vendettas, an imperious ambition and peasant's suspicion of both colleagues and opponents, a trait that had distinguished him throughout his political career but which intensified with the passage of years. He practised politics with courtly deadliness. He was long-sighted, astute and thorough in preparation for the furtherance of his aims, implacable in his determination. He trampled over the top of those who got in the way of his advancement or views unless they were too big for immediate, direct confrontation when he either bided his time patiently, waiting for a more propitious moment, or went around them to achieve by tactics what he could not win by massive strength. Inconspicuous in bestowing loyalty, he demanded it unquestioningly of others. He imparted a parsonical flavour to his condemnation of colleagues who departed from the rigid political code he mentally fixed for their observance, but for himself exercised the right to operate untrammelled by formal political conventions. He acquired the public image of a man serene, detached, judicial and disinterested, but his personal record was one of turbulence and ruthless involvement.*[102]

Reid's euphemism of the "Corsican" temperament of the Country Party leader is eloquent but the bluntness of Peter Robinson, another journalist, might be closer: *"he was a mixture between a great man and a gangster"*.[103] McEwen did operate a bit like a gangster, gathering intelligence and crushing those who crossed him, even if it took time. He had remarkable overt power, but he exercised perhaps even greater covert power. McEwen was a master in the dark arts of politics but somehow managed never to appear as a man who operated in the shadows. McEwen amassed power bureaucratically, culturally and politically, not for its own sake, but to utilize it judiciously in the national interest, which for McEwen meant what was best for the Country Party.

Power of Communication

> *"All of us who worked with him can remember his standing here at the dispatch box jangling coins in his pocket and gazing across the table from under his Mephistophelean*[104] *eyebrows but using words in a simple, direct and accurate way. He was a quite outstanding person in this Parliament in the power of his oratory and his efficacy".*[105]

McEwen also instinctively understood the power of the press in a liberal democracy. Whether it was the new national broadsheet, *The Australian* published by the ambitious and brash young Rupert Murdoch; the never-ending ideological battle with the then Australian Broadcasting Commission (ABC); through to personal and bitter feuds with individual journalists in the Canberra press gallery or the absolute necessity to stay in contact with rural communities through local rural newspapers and radio; McEwen's interest in media bordered on paranoia. Getting it wrong could have devastating consequences, as in other areas of his work life, for McEwen, preparation was everything. Press conferences of the era show a steely jawed McEwen in command of the detail and control of the dialogue, dealing with questions calmly exuding confidence, his speech was deep and resounding with memorable sibilance.

McEwen formed a deep, reciprocal and strategic alliance with the Murdoch family that began in the World War Two when Sir Keith Murdoch oversaw wartime communications on the recommendation of McEwen when he was part of Chifley's war cabinet. Young Rupert Murdoch saw McEwen as a mentor and had also deliberately cultivated the relationship in order to have his own 'trusted insider' in Canberra. McEwen was the one; it was a relationship that served both men well. It was McEwen who assisted the young publisher to purchase his London newspapers. He also assisted in the purchase of a private property just outside Yass where aspiring prime ministers and opposition leaders (except notably Bill Shorten) have subjected themselves to a pre-election interview with Murdoch. Whilst Menzies was known to have a close professional relationship with Packer, McEwen's relationship with the Murdoch family ensured he also had a trusted conduit to amplify his message to the Australian people.[106]

McEwen's views on the ABC were strident, knowing the powerful role it plays in informing country people. During his tenure, the ABC was the only public broadcaster and for the vast majority of country people, the only source of radio and television, bringing the world into the loungerooms and milking sheds across the country. However, McEwen was adamant that the ABC and sections of the media treated the Country Party unfairly particularly during federal elections campaigns. The most glaring example was during two visits to Western Australia during the 1966 federal election campaign to support two Country Party MPs who were running against Liberal candidates in three cornered contests. Deputy Prime Minister McEwen arrived in Western Australia and gave several interviews, held press conferences, spoke at public meetings where over a thousand people attended, but his presence in the West was not mentioned by the ABC in any of its coverage. Observed McEwen, *"It seemed to me that the ABC made a calculated decision to suppress any reference of my visit to Western Australia"*.[107] This was despite the ABC being in attendance at the various press conferences and his visits being widely reported by commercial television, newspapers and radio.

The local Echuca *Riverine Herald*, Western Australia's *The Countryman* or Victoria's *Weekly Times*, were all critical to McEwen's desire to demonstrate how the Country Party was delivering for the industries and communities of regional Australia. Perhaps this is because in regional towns the local paper would be read and re-read, the sole source of sharing community news, sporting successes and stock prices. In Canberra, journalists' favour was courted with a quiet whiskey and a game of snooker; he would have his favorites who benefited from the usual practice of drops of exclusive information. Journalists such as Max Newton who publicly denounced McEwen, his policies and his party were iced. Murdoch actually sacked Newton as his editor of *The Australian* because of his attacks on McEwen. This war was to culminate in front page stories during his time as Prime Minister that would destroy two careers - more on this later.

Challenged by changing technology, as television was rolled out across the country, McEwen was concerned about his image and its potential to be manipulated. The Hon. Bill Baxter, former campaign chair of McEwen's final election in 1969 recalls that the Country Party campaign launch at the Shepparton Star Theatre was the first to include the TV cameras. For the three weeks preceding the launch, McEwen would ring Bill every day to check that he had arranged to have the front 20 rows filled with local Country Party branch members. McEwen refused to have anything but rapturous applause to the speech launching the Country Party election campaign for national news bulletins. He was determined not to be heckled on television in the nightly news.[108]

Knowledge is Power

Being a self-taught, self-made man, McEwen keenly felt the lack of a formal education, but he bought a wealth of lived experience to his role that also developed over time, and a great depth of reading particularly history. He had some natural advantages such as a "phenomenal memory of relevant material" and was better read than most realised. He also possessed a clarity of thought and diligence in thinking critically about issues before him late into the evening. As he said, "*Education is a most useful basis for thinking, but education is no substitute for thinking*".[109]

It was McEwen's work ethic, dedication to using research and data that underpinned his clear and concise decision making. As Crawford recalled, he was a demanding minister who would not suffer poor or ill thought out advice from department officials. He went into negotiations at home or abroad knowing what he wanted and what his fall back positions were. He often had drafted several alternative sets of speeches or speaking notes with him, preparing for any eventuality that may arise in a given trade discussion. It was this character trait that often caught the other side by surprise.[110]

The National Party's Queensland Premier, Joh Bjelke-Petersen, was impressed by the respect and regard in which McEwen was held internationally. Bjelke-Petersen attended the 1968 international sugar agreement negotiations in Geneva on behalf of the sugar state. As he recalled to Golding:

> *There was no question that McEwen was the dominant force in the conference ... Under his desk he would have a number of different speeches ready for any eventuality. Sometimes he would pull out one speech and then put it back and take out another one if the argument suddenly went in another direction.*[111]

Intergenerational Power

For McEwen, there was no point in holding and wielding power as an individual. Rather, as leader this was done for the benefit of the Country Party and so it must extend beyond his tenure. By contast, without the towering Menzies the pickings in the Liberal Party were slim as Menzies had groomed only Holt for leader. The next generation of Country Party leaders must be able to continue the fight after McEwen was gone. And so, McEwen was a great mentor for the talented young men coming up through the ranks. McEwen had closely mentored four potential successors, any of whom had the potential to be leaders. They were to be blooded during the post-Holt leadership crisis.

As McEwen recalled:

> *The situation is, I said, that I am the Country Party. This is bloody well not safe and has got to be ended. The Country Party cannot depend on one man and be floundering if it loses that man. You have got to build up behind me more than we have now." In preparation for my own retirement, I carefully selected adequate lieutenants. I was at pains over a period of ten years or so to arrange a line of succession behind me. I was quite tough and ruthless in passing over good men to put in people with greater potential. If (Anthony, Sinclair, Nixon or Hunt) had been available at one point in time, I would not like to have had to judge between them. I regard the four of them as being pretty much on the same level.*[112]

Larry Anthony, Doug Anthony's son and himself later a federal parliamentarian and minister, remembers how McEwen closely and carefully managed the growth and development of this group of young men that included his father Doug who eventually succeeded McEwen as the Country Party leader in 1971:

> *Menzies wanted to make my father Minister for the Navy but McEwen said to Menzies, 'No, no, you can't have young Doug as Minister for the Navy because he is too young and they wouldn't respect him. He needs a portfolio where he can get into it.' He was then made Minister for Interior where he could thrive, following in the footsteps of McEwen.*[113]

McEwen also encouraged his protégées when they made a mistake. Nixon tells a story that shows McEwen's compassionate leadership style:

> *In the joint Party meeting, we were debating setting up the wool commission,"* Nixon recalls, *"I was a backbencher and I got fired up on it and I made some mistakes in my presentation. I quoted wrong figures. And it was only by accident, I knew the right figures. Menzies used to sit there with a pen and doodling on the desk. He never looked up unless somebody said something ridiculous. All of a sudden Menzies looked up and it took the wind right out of my sail. I sat down, it wasn't 500 million, it was 5,000 million. Well, something like that. I was upset as hell. I was quite disturbed that I've made this silly mistake and made myself look a fool. But as we were walking down the corridor, John McEwen picked me up, John McEwen came out of the partyroom and raced up to put his arm around my shoulder and he said, 'you might have learned something there today, don't quote wrong figures!' John said. And I said, 'I won't, and I'll be back next week.' And John said, 'good'. So, I mean, he helped you when you made a mistake and he'd encourage you to have another go, which I did the next week.*[114]

McEwen knew that being powerful was not just about being the loudest or the strongest and that silence could also yield powerful results. Sinclair speaks about how McEwen imparted this wisdom to all of his young lieutenants about how using silence or being judicious with the timing of your intervention could have devastating effects. As Sinclair remembered: *"He had considerable capacity to choose his moments for intervention in a way that meant his words were very consequential in determining the outcome. So, his timing for intervention of debating was impeccable and effective".*[115]

And as Nixon recalls:

> *I went into my first cabinet submission. As you know, the Treasurer was always the first to speak and then they'd go round the table. And then the minister had final say. Billy McMahon was Treasurer and Billy really climbed all over us. I was sitting on the edge of a chair, ready to fight. I was fired up, ready to go. And McEwen who sat next to the Prime Minister flicked his hand over his shoulder, his thumb over his shoulder. 'Let it go.' And I just sort of sagged, and I sat back in my chair, and McMahon wound up and Menzies said, 'I think you've got that Peter.' As we were going out the door, John McEwen came over to me, he said, 'I think you might have learned something there today. He said, there's a time to speak and a time to be silent.'* [116]

Former Deputy Prime Minister and later leader of the Nationals, Doug Anthony said:

> *McEwen was my mentor. He was certainly the most adroit politician that I have known. Whilst I loved to listen to Menzies, I was engrossed by McEwen's political techniques. These I witnessed with farming groups, industrialists and journalists, as well as in international discussions. He had an ability to assess the wisest approach for each audience.*[117]

From the floor of the House of Representatives on the occasion of McEwen's death[118] Ian Sinclair spoke of childless

McEwen's patient paternal relationship with his young Country Party ministers:

> *Basically, the strength of John McEwen lay in his ability to recruit and to use the talents of others. He had an extraordinary ability to get the best out of people. He was certainly one who gave loyalty and expected loyalty...essentially, he was a father to us all.*[119]

***

The Power Struggle

Anyone in Canberra in the 1960s remembers the great power struggle between Treasury and McEwen's behemoth Department of Trade and Industry. But the debate and competition for influence over policy was not necessarily a bad thing. Financial Editor of the *Sydney Morning Herald* on 5 January 1968 wrote:

> *In good Sir Robert's golden days, Mr McEwan (sic) stood as an activist and a man of independent mind in the Cabinet. Until the 1960s he was very much in the running as a possible successor to the Prime Minister; he had not yet arrived at the banks of the Rubicon which forced him to the decision on electoral boundaries that alienated the Liberals. While the hopes of ultimate leadership were evidently a restraining factor, Mr McEwen was nevertheless accomplishing bold and novel things on the trade front. The Japanese Trade Agreement was splendidly in tune with history, or rather just the right distance ahead to mould history.*
>
> *The tensions of those days between the Department and*

> the Treasury were fruitful tensions over genuine issues. The negativism of the Treasury was rampant in the early 1960s. Mr McEwen's pragmatic line, his doer's disrespect for precedent were often of real service to the country.

The points of dispute between Trade and Treasury were not, as might be expected, about tariffs, but other issues. When Harold Holt was the Treasurer, he clashed with McEwen on many topics including on foreign investment, the devaluation of the currency, and the establishment of the Australian Industry Development Corporation, known by some as the 'McEwen Bank'. Devaluation of the currency was always a hot topic in Canberra. Those who argued against devaluation, most of the Liberals, argued on grounds of increasing foreign investment into Australia, whereas those who supported it, like McEwen and his party, pointed to the prospective bad effects on exports for both secondary industry and commodities. McEwen and Menzies usually worked well together but the two had clashed fiercely on currency devaluation in the so-called 'battle for the pound' and McEwen, as was his habit, got his way. But in 1968 the topic was before Cabinet again following Britain's Wilson's Labour Government's 16 per cent devaluation of the pound sterling. "A Special Correspondent" at *The Australian* wrote just after it happened:

> ...(McEwen) reacts — some say overreacts — to the alarm bells of international trade. Mr McEwen still believes that British devaluation constitutes a basic threat to Australia's export of manufactured goods. He came out for corresponding Australian devaluation. The late Prime Minister (Holt) opposed him, so did the rest of Cabinet. The argument went on with McEwen sticking

> to his guns. Britain's increased export competitiveness, he said, would lead to a plea for higher tariffs at a time when the price of domestic and imported goods are up, with wage increases likely to follow. Characteristically, he let off another broadside at Mr Holt when he enquired, in effect, if the International Monetary Fund HAD been asked whether it would have approved Australian devaluation.[120]

It is interesting to note the nature of McEwen's arguments. One who allegedly worshipped at the altar of the tariff would probably not have pointed to the prospect of rising tariffs as a result of failing to match Britain's devaluation of the pound as a possible negative outcome. Nevertheless, McEwen for once lost that fight. Harold Holt got a glorious win in Cabinet against the Deputy Prime Minister just days before his fateful swim at Cheviot Beach. As Peter Golding pointed out, Holt, on the back of a great political win in Canberra, may have felt overconfident that day as he stared from the shore out to the dangerous waters.

Holt and McEwen's policy rivalries never developed into a personal rivalry. But McEwen's relationship with Billy McMahon was one of true mutual hatred. Yet it was not always so. McMahon was once McEwen's junior minister for Primary Industries in 1956 (this department was under the umbrella of Trade and Industry at the time) and the pair had a good working relationship initially. But things soon got uncomfortable when McEwen returned from Great Britain with a renegotiated Ottawa Agreement to find that the deal's press release had gone out under the name (junior) Minister William McMahon. McEwen never got to the bottom of who made this 'mistake', but he had a suspicion and McMahon was marked out as one to keep an eye on ever after.

McMahon was more economically liberal than McEwen; he particularly did not want McEwen to get his industry development bank, noting the Coalition had got into government in the first place all those years ago by defeating Ben Chifley's attempt to nationalise Australia's private banks. But the two men's rivalry was much more about personalities and power than policy. McMahon saw McEwen as an obstacle to his ultimate goal — the prime ministership. Both McMahon and McEwen were orphaned, but that was where the similarities ended. McMahon was an anathema to McEwen — a wealthy city boy, gregarious, cheeky and a partygoer. He was a small man, balding, with a soft lilting voice and big pointy ears. He could be shallow and was attracted to the trappings of power and privilege. At 57 McMahon famously married 32-year-old glamorous socialite Sonia Hopkins. Notably, McMahon owned an apartment at Kings Cross, Sydney's premier nightlife strip and cultivated a coterie of dubious characters around him. One such character particularly disquieted McEwen - the brilliant economic journalist, Maxwell Newton. In a recent speech, Paul Kelly said Newton *"had a head full of Adam Smith and talked like a wharfie,"*[121] but this doesn't really capture the truly extraordinary, chaotic persona of this iconoclast. As previously mentioned, for a period of McEwen's life, Newton became almost an obsession and the feeling was mutual. In the 1960s John McEwen made it his mission to destroy him - but Newton started it.

As previously stated, genuine opposition to *McEwenism* was still rare among the Liberal and Labor parties, but in the mid-1960s,' Young Turk' Free Traders like John Stone were beginning to rise through Treasury's ranks, and as Paul Kelly has pointed out, "economically literate and aggressive journalists"[122] were emerging at newspapers up and down the country. There was Alan Wood and Ken Davidson at *The Australian* and Maximillian Walsh at the *Australian Financial Review* — but Maxwell Newton stood above them all. Newton was considered an economics prodigy by Cambridge dons when he studied there, and his analyses were beginning to hurt McEwen. As Paul Kelly has said:

> In a directive worthy of a place in the history of our politics and journalism Max Newton, Editor of the Financial Review sent Alan Wood to Canberra in the early 1960s telling him: "Take on tariffs as an issue. We're going to pull this bloody McEwen on." P.P. McGuinness, a subsequent Financial Review Editor said: 'What Newton did was point Australian economic journalism in a new direction, looking at the economic issues and corruption surrounding the use of the tariff system.' Wood said: 'My instructions were to develop a tariff round because Newton considered it an important national policy issue and no newspaper was covering it.' Alan's middle initial was 'T' for Thomas, but he quickly became known as Alan "Tariff" Wood. Many colleagues were amused by his 'incomprehensible activities' – but not all of them.[123]

At this time, Newton started writing stories with startling scoops that could only have come from Cabinet leaks. There was a lot of anger and finger pointing in the Holt Cabinet. McEwen had a pretty good idea where the leaks were coming from. Peter Nixon has said that McMahon was known as a "professional leaker".[124] McEwen lost all trust in the Treasurer; they became enemies. It was a portent of an extraordinary feud between the two powerful men that would come to a head in tragic circumstances in a battle to lead the nation.

***

Most Australians know that we had a Prime Minister who went out for a swim and was never seen again, but the dark intrigue and plotting in the shadows is a lesser-known story. There are few days in Australian politics more remarkable than those that followed Harold Holt's solo swim at Portsea. This is an astonishing period in Australian history. For one thing, it spelt an end to our naivety; never again would an Australian leader be left alone to do their own thing.

In the subsequent days, as the extraordinary events unfolded over the wireless and on black and white televisions around the country, behind closed doors the brutal nature of Australian politics rose to the surface. In the chaotic hours, days and weeks that followed the disappearance, ambitious men jostled for power at an undignified pace. Don Chipp, one time Liberal Minister and later founder of the Australian Democrats, said that the atmosphere in St Paul's Cathedral for Holt's memorial was "sickening" and some of the mourners were "unspeakable bastards".[125] Senior government ministers, departmental heads, journalists and public figures were all making urgent, frenetic manoeuvres, vying for control and there stood McEwen in the midst of it all, holding the drafting gate. He was unmatched in skill, in reading the political mood, in his foresight, planning and future proofing, and in his strength of will. Significantly, these events lay bare his ambition and ruthlessness. Almost certainly, in this moment McEwen realised that his time had come, that if he wanted the top job it was now or never. And he was ready to fight. The prospect seems a little extraordinary today, vainglorious even, but in 1967 the Liberal Party was adolescent, struggling to find its post-Menzies identity, and not yet steeped in a vast political tradition. Small 'l' liberals had only just begun to organise. The Country Party was older, wiser and knew who it was and what it stood for and its leader was popular, respected and the most experienced man in the government. However, there was another man, a smaller man, the most able man the Liberals had at that time, who also emerged determined to seize what he apparently saw as his birthright. William McMahon wanted the keys to the Lodge and he wanted them desperately.

It is not widely known that the day Holt went missing, there were two letters found inside his abandoned briefcase at the beach house revealing an extraordinary vice-regal intervention into national politics. One letter was from McMahon and the other from the Governor-General, Sir Richard Casey. The letters contained two very different accounts of a single meeting between the two men. In the preceding months, the enmity between Holt's Deputy Prime Minister and his Treasurer had become so bitter, the leaking so regular and damaging, that the Prime Minister having tried and failed to mediate himself, had sought the intercession of the Governor-General. Holt needed to get to the bottom of why his two most able ministers were at each other's throats. Casey obliged and requested McMahon visit him. They had a frank discussion lasting for nearly two hours at Admiralty House, overlooking the Sydney Harbour and the Sydney Opera House with its sails still covered in iron scaffolding. The journalist Maxwell Newton was a central topic of conversation. Here is an excerpt from the Governor-General's letter to Prime Minister Holt, dated 9 December:

> *I had a long talk alone with McMahon at Admiralty House, at my request, yesterday morning... I said that his (McMahon's) present notorious relationship with McEwen rubbed off on the relationships between the Liberal and Country Parties – and so was to be deplored, as it reduced the prestige of the Government in the public mind and so might well affect the Election results.*
>
> *I then spoke of his apparent close relationship with Maxwell Newton and the latter's public writings in support of him (McMahon) and in denigration of McEwen and indeed yourself. I said that Newton had had a certain reputation with responsible people, some of whom had conveyed their disapprobation of him (Newton) to me.*
>
> *I also spoke of his (McMahon's) having taken Newton with him on two overseas conferences, which he (McMahon) denied. He said that Newton had travelled at his own expense to these overseas conferences, and not even in the same aircraft as himself (McMahon) and, at the conferences, had received no more than normal press contact with him (McMahon). He (McMahon) denied any close relationship with Newton and said that he (Newton) had never received any inside information from him. It was noticeable that he referred to Newton as 'Max' throughout.* [126]

The letter goes on to reveal that McEwen had confided in Casey his thoughts of retiring:

> *I said that in my personal contacts with McEwen I had tried to argue privately for his remaining in the Parliament for as long as possible so as to postpone the day when a younger Country Party man would replace him which would inevitably raise problems with the Liberal Party about the Deputy prime ministership. By his (McMahon's) relationship with McEwen, he had kept McEwen in a degree of nervous tension which affected his health and so menaced his remaining in Parliament. He (McMahon) said that any conflict with McEwen originated with McEwen and not with himself.*[127]

The second letter from McMahon to Holt dated 11 December had a decidedly different version of the same events and McMahon took issue with the constitutional legitimacy of Casey's intervention but:

> *His Excellency said he thought he had a Constitutional responsibility to serve the Government in power, whether it was Liberal or Labour(sic), and he had to do his best to see that the Government functioned effectively.*[128]

Notably, despite the objective of the meeting being to discover the nature of the relationship between Newton and McMahon, McMahon's account to the Prime Minister omitted any mention of the name Newton:

> *The Governor-General talked to me about several matters. It was very much a repetition of the discussions between yourself, Mr. McEwen and others and myself on the 8th November 1967. The discussion could well be valuable. It was frank and wide ranging. At the end His Excellency said on two occasions that he had been badly*

*informed and on one occasion said: "God! I have been misinformed on this too."*¹²⁹

It was summer break, coming up on Christmas. Prime Minister Holt may never have had time to read these letters. Yet certainly, as he swam out into the riptide, he left on the shore a titanic clash unresolved.

When McEwen first heard that the Prime Minister was missing, he was home at *Chilgala*. He received a phone call from his friend, the wife of airline heir Bob Ansett who had heard it on the wireless. McEwen immediately swung into action — there would be no doubt who was in charge. The first thing McEwen did was contact the Governor-General. As former ministerial colleagues Casey and McEwen had a good relationship; in fact, Casey's trust in McEwen was forged in the fire of World War Two. McEwen informed him that, given the circumstances, he would be heading to Canberra immediately and would contact him again later in the day. McEwen next called Dame Zara Holt, who assured McEwen that her husband was a strong swimmer and that she was confident he would be found safe. McEwen also spoke to the laconic Sir Peter Lawler, head of the Department of the Prime Minister who was less confident, *"I think the PM's a gonner... I think we are without a prime minister"*.¹³⁰

McEwen arranged to head to Canberra that early afternoon from a tiny airstrip in Mangalore, an hour's drive away. Significantly, he recalled his chief lieutenants Doug Anthony, Peter Nixon and Ian Sinclair to join him in Canberra. Nixon remembers the day vividly — he was himself out at sea, fishing off Cape Conran in far East

Gippsland and received a call on the two-way radio. McEwen actually sent a chartered plane to pick Anthony up from Coolangatta, on the Gold Coast, Queensland. Both men arrived in Canberra the afternoon of the 17th ready for deployment. Sinclair would also eventually join them too, after a hospital vigil for his extremely ill wife.

On that afternoon, John McEwen also issued a press statement as the Deputy Prime Minister from his own office, rather than accessing the Prime Minister's advisers. The statement sought to reassure a shocked nation that a full-scale search and rescue operation for Holt was underway and that all Australians would be *"praying that he would be found safe and sound"*.[131] Meanwhile, McEwen was preparing for the worst.

It is clear that McEwen was not wasting time waiting to see what may play out and had accepted the advice of Lawler that the Prime Minister was dead. McEwen was determined to fix the result of the ensuing power struggle — ensuring the outcome was in the best interests of the Country Party and the nation. As already said, for McEwen, these were never mutually exclusive.

Over a long and tense supper at Government House in Yarralumla that same Sunday evening, McEwen provided the Governor-General with advice on a pathway through the crisis. Importantly, McEwen made clear from the outset he would not serve under a McMahon prime ministership. Recalling the discussions that took place on that fateful afternoon, Sinclair stated *"McEwen didn't trust McMahon at all,"*[132] while Nixon added, *"We all shared McEwen's distrust of him"*.[133] The message being sent was crystal clear — the

Australian Government would fall, as the Country Party would withdraw its support, if it was to be led by a man who had consistently undermined both the Country Party's leader and its policy positions.

No doubt Casey and McEwen discussed history that night; this kind of brinkmanship was not without precedent in Australian politics. Former Country Party leader Earle Page had tried to veto Menzies' rise to the prime ministership 28 years earlier creating enormous instability. Having both been there in 1939, the consequential destabilisation of the then UAP Government was an outcome McEwen and Casey sought not to repeat. Ever the patriot McEwen chose to forewarn the Governor-General of his veto on McMahon, rather than let a process take place that would end in a fallen government.

Meanwhile, McMahon, who was entertaining friends at his posh home in Sydney, on hearing of Holt's disappearance, canvassed with them the prospect of him running for the Liberal leadership. McMahon too had requested a VIP aircraft to get him down to Canberra early that afternoon. But while McEwen did not hesitate, McMahon blinked. He did board the plane but on receipt of sound advice from his press secretary Peter Kelly, *"that if he did the press would run stories that he arrived in Canberra even before the body was cold' 'but Jack is already there!"*[134] a rattled McMahon exclaimed. The Treasurer was experienced enough to understand that despite being the Deputy Leader of Liberal Party and hence the presumptive successor, he sensed powerful forces were gathering on the ground against him. McMahon's instincts were right. They were working hard and fast to ensure he did not become the next prime minister.

Earlier in the day McEwen had discussed the prospect of Paul Hasluck as a "stable team man"[135] and as such his preferred option for Liberal leader, but he later became *"astonished and dismayed "*[136] that Hasluck had declared a reticence to canvass for votes. Hasluck failed to understand that to lead a political party is not an hereditary right to be bestowed without a fight, 'merit unheralded' was an anathema to McEwen. For McEwen, it was a privilege, granted by peers who should be convinced of your merit, desire and character. McEwen had to wait 19 years to become leader of his own party and hence Deputy Prime Minister and understood instinctively that if Hasluck was not going to fight to be prime minister, he would not win. As Nixon remembers, "McEwen spoke to Paul Hasluck and said you'll have to start ringing around and Hasluck said, I'm not going to ask for one vote. He said, *"they know me. I don't need to ring around"*. *McEwen came back to the office and said,* "Paul Hasluck can't win it".[137]

If not Hasluck then who else could they back to block McMahon? The Country Party ministers identified Senator John Gorton, former Country Party member and then Government Senate Leader, and Minister for Education and Science as a possible compromise candidate. Putting up a senator was unheard of and it would take time and require several procedural and possible constitutional obstacles to overcome. It was not a perfect solution, but it had the added bonus of giving McEwen more time in power.

McEwen dispatched his deputy, Doug Anthony to Gorton's house in Narrabundah, Canberra to tell him to put his name forward. A pyjamaed Gorton was surprised at a late evening knock on the door from Anthony. So awoken from sleep, whilst the search for Prime Minister Holt was still being conducted, Gorton was told by Anthony, on behalf of 'Black Jack' McEwen that the Country Party had drafted him to become the Liberal Party leader and he would have their full backing. An astonished and incredulous Gorton must not have gone back to sleep, preparing his own ambitious plan for how to secure the top job which as a Senator, he would never have previously contemplated.

Less than 12 hours from first hearing of the Prime Minister Holt's disappearance, McEwen had developed a fully-fledged battle plan, set up a command post in Canberra, swung his key lieutenants into action, gathered intelligence which would even extend to state counterintelligence. Nixon's job was to be a spy and go drinking with the Liberals to find out what was going on from their perspective – a role he took seriously:

> Then he (McEwen) said to me 'you go to the ante room every night and have a beer with the boys'. Well I used to go to the anteroom every night, half past 4 and they were talking down there about who was going to replace Harold and I just wanted to sit in on all the gossip... All the Liberal ministers used to gather there, and I was just the quiet boy in the corner. I was able to report back to him...Nobody loved McMahon and when a statement came out that we were going to block him - there was a bit of whoopee.[138]

This was McEwen's pinnacle moment and he seized it. It would require all his political skills, honed over many decades to get the right outcome. Early Monday morning, learning from Page's mistake, McEwen rang all Country

Party MPs to ascertain their support for the position he was taking. Not surprisingly, he had their full support.

McEwen then told McMahon to his face – as men of the country do – that he would not serve under him if he were to succeed in winning the Liberal leadership. *"Bill, I won't serve under you because I don't trust you."*[139] One key to the Coalition's stability and electoral success (irrespective of its parties' differing views on policy) had been the matter of trust between the leaders of the Liberal and Country parties. Their success was based on a pact, that both parties were independent, each serving unique and separate constituencies despite areas of overlap, and that the nation's interests were served in having both parties in government. As McEwen said, *"McMahon seemed to me to be a threat to the Coalition. He was one of those people in the Liberal Party who felt they would be better off if there was no Country Party to contend with"*.[140]

Importantly, McEwen also let his Liberal Cabinet colleagues know that if he were commissioned to the prime ministership he would stand aside as soon as the Liberals selected their new leader. McMahon was hoping for a quick party room meeting prior to Christmas to elect a new leader. This move would have most likely meant McEwen would remain "acting prime minister" rather than being sworn in.

That afternoon, Monday the 18th, McEwen formally advised the Governor-General of his views as the acting Prime Minister, specifically the unfair advantage any Liberal MP promoted to the role in an acting capacity would receive in any future leadership ballot. He determinedly requested that the Governor-General should therefore *"make me Prime*

Minister ".[141]

McEwen would not countenance any constrictions or conditions on a commission to be prime minister. If drafted, he expected to be sworn in with the full authority of the position. Casey, meanwhile, had sought advice from both Attorney-General, Nigel Bowen, and Sir Garfield Barwick Chief Justice of the High Court, regarding the precedent set by commissioning the deputy prime minister, leader of the minority Coalition party, rather than the direct line of leadership succession, the deputy leader of the majority party. Bowen and Barwick both concluded that if Holt was not found, McEwen should become prime minister until the Liberals elected a new leader. It wasn't just the Country Party blocking McMahon; Liberal Minister Hasluck had also formally advised the Governor-General that he would not serve in a McMahon ministry. Hasluck then rang Gorton to encourage him to run. It seemed nobody wanted McMahon, and this bad news was relayed to McMahon in an afternoon meeting by the Governor-General. McMahon was not surprised. Round 1 McEwen.

The conclusion of McEwen's elaborate plans to reach the pinnacle of Australian politics is covered in *Prime Minister*.

Power in the shadows

The powers of authority of high office are transparent and, in a liberal democracy such as Australia, come with public accountability. And while this overt power is well understood, great men require the ability to also harness covert power. Over many decades, McEwen built a network of contacts and connections in and outside of government to provide critical information to execute his agenda. There was a surface level power struggle between McEwen and McMahon, Trade and Treasury, played publicly through the press and openly spoken about in the halls of parliament house. There was also a quiet and yet more brutal power struggle in the shadows. McEwen believed that his political enemy was potentially exposed to questions of compromise to national security in the highest offices of the nation.

Once again, Maxwell Newton, prominent journalist and later brothel proprietor, was central to these events. Interestingly, Newton attended the Perth Modern School in the same class as Bob Hawke, John Stone and Rolf Harris, and he also brought Marvel comics to Australia. Newton's daughter described him follows:

> *In the late 1970s Sir John Gorton, one-time Prime Minister, publicly stated that Maxwell Newton was the cause of his downfall, while simultaneously in Melbourne, Federal Police unsuccessfully attempted to pin charges on Maxwell Newton of selling hard pornography - as he sat underneath a gigantic fake chandelier at his desk, in the office of one of his brothels, saying the Alcoholics' Anonymous 'Twelve Steps' with an old journo mate. Also at that time, Maxwell Newton had filed for bankruptcy, his debts amounting to $6.1 million. In the 1980s he was living in America, a wealthy man whose economic analyses had won the praise of Milton Friedman.*[142]

When stories emerged that Newton had struck up a friendship with McMahon, every alarm bell must have been going off in McEwen's head. Newton was a great womaniser, a husband to three wives and father of six children but the friendship he developed with Billy McMahon was very close. According to Newton's daughter:

> ...on a personal level Maxwell found McMahon to be very good value and often took the micky out of him with friends, mimicking McMahon mincing and teetering around with his little watering can and wearing his 'lederhosen'. Once, at Hotel Canberra, McMahon came up behind Maxwell sitting at a table, and, putting his hands over Maxwell's eyes, whispered coyly in a singsong voice, 'Who is it?'"[143]

Clyde Packer once wrote: "McMahon started toting Newton around wherever he went. On one occasion, Newton was arrested in Trinidad at a Commonwealth Finance Ministers' conference for swiping a British working paper and was going to be thrown off the island. McMahon interceded and had him released."[144]

Further documents in Holt's briefcase contain an allegation that funds from McMahon's Treasury Department had been used to pay for Maxwell Newton's trip to Rio de Janeiro for meetings of the International Monetary Fund (IMF) and the World Bank, that Newton had been on the "British tab" whilst staying in London, and further that the United States Information Service, the international public relations agency of the US government had paid for internal flights during Newton's trip to the United States, and that flights to and from Australia "were paid by Treasury".[145] McMahon rejected some of these assertions in a letter to Prime Minister Holt, stating that Newton was not accredited by the IMF and received "no assistance whatsoever" from Treasury.[146]

In 1969, McEwen and Newton's rivalry reached boiling point when a diplomatic cable from Paris leaked out of McEwen's Trade Department and was printed in Newton's *Incentive* newsletter. As John Stone recalls, *"(Newton) was doing well enough to be bribing a couple of people, ...(one) in the Department of Trade and Industry was slipping in copies of cables ... Anyway, McEwen was determined to find out what the hell was going on, where these leaks were coming from. And he set the dogs onto Max."*[147] On the 23rd of May 1969, Commonwealth Police officers swooped on Maxwell Newton's home and office in Deakin, Canberra. Not content to simply search desks and filing cabinets, over eleven hours ten officers went through beds, cupboards, stoves, and toilets. "Anyway, they must have found some things that were enough to lay a charge on Max," Stone continues, "which McEwen very gleefully did".[148] This story is on the public record, but one detail is not. According to John Stone, Newton told him that during breakfast one morning Newton's phone rang and *"there was a little squeaky voice at the other end speaking very quickly saying CHECK THE WARRANTS! CHECK THE WARRANTS! He knew straight away that it was Billy"*.[149] John Stone goes on to surmise that McEwen must have mentioned in a recent Cabinet meeting that the warrant for Newton's arrest was defective and McMahon rushed off to inform his accomplice. Following the phone call, Newton had his lawyers check the validity of the warrants and it turns out that they were defective, and the charges were dropped.

Omitted from McEwen's autobiography are two meetings which occurred during his prime ministership. One was with young Rupert Murdoch on January 4th 1968. The other was with the Director-General of ASIO, Brigadier Sir Charles Spry or 'Scorpion'.[150] Even though McEwen had blocked McMahon's run for the prime ministership publicly following Holt's death, there were still loose ends. This was a man that did his own dirty work. Using his contacts, built up over time he called in his favours from the Press Gallery and our national intelligence agency.

In the weeks that followed, editorials in Packer mastheads discussing the Liberal leadership contenders tended to be sympathetic to McMahon, whereas Murdoch's *The Australian* championed McEwen: *"he has the capacity; he has the experience; he has the knowledge* (to deny him because) *he belongs to the minority part of the coalition* (would be contrary to) *the national interest"*.[151]

Each backed their man to succeed. McEwen was not taking any chances as public opinion swung behind the 'hard done by' McMahon. Months previously, McEwen had facilitated the unearthing of concerning national security revelations about a close confidant of McMahon — his media nemesis, economics journalist and anti-tariff possessed Maxwell Newton. It must be revealed to the public that McMahon was not fit to be prime minister if his closest confidants were national security risks. And so, McEwen called young Rupert to the Kurrajong Hotel for a quiet chat.

An editorial by a 'Special Correspondent' (widely assumed to be Murdoch himself) extolled the virtues of McEwen remaining as prime minister. Meanwhile, *The Australian* on January 6 described concerns about a close associate of McMahon who was "an agent of foreign interest", in an article titled "Why McEwen vetoed McMahon". Similarly, the front page of Fairfax's *Sydney Morning Herald* two days later outlined security concerns of the allegations against McMahon. Remember, when Australians were reading these stories, it was the height of the Cold War, the Petrov affair (1954-55) was only a decade ago and Australia was at war in Vietnam. Middle aged Australians had worn a uniform in their youth or loved someone who had. Our outlook and security were important to us, we realised how far away allies were and how close the threats. We took national security seriously.

McEwen had another undocumented meeting with 'Scorpion'. The topic? An agency investigation of Newton. During the two decades following World War Two ASIO had grown into an impressive organisation even giving the KGB a run for their Ruble. As with many other similar agencies during the height of the Cold War throughout the 1960s and 1970s, looking for enemies, subjects of interest, at home was routine. McEwen's own Secretary of Trade, Alan Westerman, drew ASIO's attention to the actions of the Japan Export Trade Organisation (JETRO), and the organisation's contractual relationship with Newton. An additional memo from 'Scorpion' claimed that this *"indicated the possibility of subversion"*[152] by the Japanese Government in Australian domestic affairs through the medium of Newton. The title of the file was "SPOILING OPERATIONS — Newton, Maxwell".[153]

According to a declassified Top Secret ASIO memo, the article that appeared in *The Australian* with the claim that Maxwell Newton was an agent of foreign interest, was written following the direct instruction of Rupert Murdoch. According to the memo, some of his information was *"believed to have been given to Murdoch by Mr McEwen"*.[154] Newton had previously written an article that referred to Murdoch (his former boss and now proprietor of the Australian) as that young 'whipper snapper from Adelaide'. The ASIO memo quotes an alleged phone call from Murdoch to Newton, in which the fledgling media magnate told his former editor, *"this is the whipper snapper from Adelaide. I suggest you read my paper tomorrow"* and hung up.[155]

Far sighted McEwen had a plan to discredit his nemesis Newton long before Holt's fateful disappearance, but did the plan always also include McMahon's downfall? Surely not, because how could anyone have predicted the disappearance of Harold Holt? The original request to ASIO came in August and presumably was escalated over Christmas break by the then Prime Minister McEwen. It remains an open question whether McEwen genuinely believed Newton was a real threat to national security or simply a threat to McEwen's platform and reputation.

Nevertheless, the dual benefit of this information getting into the hands of the press was that both McMahon and Newton were castrated in one action. McEwen was prepared to go there. Murdoch was prepared to go there. So was 'Scorpion'. This action highlights McEwen's ruthlessness to protect home and hearth from an enemy in every sense dangerous to the development of the regions, protection for all and the sustainability of the Country Party.

The use and accumulation of power over a political career is not about the use of force. In a democracy such as Australia, more subtle methods must be adopted. Both McEwen's physical presence and strength of will are personal characteristics which have been described as a force, but it is his use of persuasion in his exercise of political power that marks him out. When men or a number of men realise their own will in a communal action, even against the resistance of others they are said to possess power.

The accrual of power by McEwen over the course of his career is staggering. McEwen had amassed a powerful bureaucratic machine with connections across the globe; he ensured his Country Party was respected and feared and left his time in parliament having secured legal structures that would keep the Country Party at the centre of any future coalition government. Of course, there was the obvious authority that came as a result of specific roles, he also accumulated cultural and institutional power which allowed him to secure intended outcomes. As a minister, he was known to not suffer fools and woe betide the public servant who sought to obfuscate or wasn't across the brief. McEwen knew he wasn't the most educated man in the room, he relied on surrounding himself with the best and brightest of our public service. But he was unequivocal that upon hearing options, information and challenges, it was his reasonability as minister to make the final decision, a classical approach to ministerial accountability. Roles within the Trade and Industry Department were fiercely sought as a result. He used extensive knowledge to make policy decisions. He used covert information, gleaned from a vast array of sources, to inform his political strategy. This allowed him to be one step ahead of his enemies, and his friends. This information network, thanks to his time in power, reached from local Victorian Country Party branches, to global multilateral institutions. McEwen's physical characteristics which have also been described as a force. His physical bearing, and presence when he simply walked into a room conveyed the power of his strength of will, his furrowed brow, his public dark demeanour, all conveyed a latent force that he used to further the outcomes of the country and the Country Party.

Power is contained, force is the exercise of power. McEwen didn't have to rely on the exercise of force to achieve outcomes. He used silence, coalitions, time, knowledge and persuasive, grounded rhetoric. Rarely did he force the threat of bringing down the coalition government. McEwen exercised both authoritative power as Deputy PM, minister and his depth of experience, but it was his ability to affect the decisions of others through a process of persuasion where he had incredible success in cabinet, in party conferences, in international meetings that impresses.

6

PRIME MINISTER

"Unlike the Queen's representative, the prime minister is a supremely political person. In the democratic era, he is vested for a time with the full lease of the people's authority, (that) may be revoked at the next election."

– Graham Maddox, *Australian Democracy in Theory and Practice*, (Longman, 1996), p 218.

It does McEwen a great disservice to describe him as simply a 'caretaker' prime minister. For the 23 days following the disappearance of Harold Holt, he *was* the Prime Minister. Furthermore, he had also acted in the role 17 times during Menzies' prolonged absences from Australia, standing in as Prime Minister for over 500 days, sometimes for months on end. It is important to emphasise he was no stop-gap prime minister; his was a Cabinet sworn to the Queen where he exercised full authority as prime minister, without condition.

Favoring Gorton, Jeff Hook, 1967
(Jeff Hook, used with permission).

His veto of McMahon after Holt's death in 1967.
(Jeff Hook, used with permission).

Menzies himself saw McEwen as a fitting successor, whom he identified as such from as early as 1962 following the disappointing 1961 election results. This was further perpetuated by some Liberal MPs, commentators in the press over the following five years, and almost certainly through encouragement by the man himself. Indeed, McEwen was the Country Party prime minister we might have had for a much longer period, but for the fears and petty jealousies of lesser men who knew deep down he was the outstanding conservative politician of his era.

However, McEwen refused to leave the Country Party nor to entertain any merger of the coalition parties, thus creating a barrier that made it difficult for supportive Liberals to climb over. But it was a close call. The subsequent deliberate marshalling of a new generation of Liberal MPs ensured it would never happen.

The advice of McEwen's grandmother from his childhood, "If you go into politics, become the prime minister" was always going to be difficult to achieve via the minority party in the highly successful Coalition government of 1949-1972. It was to only occur through tragedy.

Tuesday December 19, 1967

Just two days after Holt was reported as missing, McEwen was sworn-in as Australia's 18th Prime Minister, attended at Government House by his three cabinet ministers, Anthony, Nixon and Sinclair. Records of the event show a nervous stern-faced McEwen entering the building and leaving with a joking, smiling group of Country Party men, posing briefly for photos and enjoying the historic moment afterwards. There was much to do and not a lot of time. Holt's memorial service was set for December 22nd. The Governor-General's statement following the swearing-in declared that *"government parties"*[156] would come together at a later date to determine the coalition leader. This terminology would have caused great consternation within the Liberal party, as it challenged the assumption that the Liberal leader would automatically lead the coalition and in government become the Prime Minister. With 27 MPs and Senators, the Country Party would be the largest faction within any joint party room meeting. This was a power move by McEwen, but it was not without precedent; the UAP and the Country Party had jointly determined the new prime minister following the 1941 resignation of Menzies during the early days of World War Two , selecting the Country Party leader and at that time Treasurer, Artie Fadden. Presumably Prime Minister McEwen's advice to the Governor-General was that the Country Party effectively had a veto power, making clear that stable government was dependent on the two separate political parties agreeing on a Prime Minister.

Meanwhile, senior Liberal ministers were meeting at Parliament House with McMahon, determined to ensure the 'McEwen Government' would be temporary. The Liberal Party leadership, which included their Senate Leader Gorton, rejected their deputy leader McMahon's suggestion for an early party meeting as 'unseemly' in the present circumstances. Preferring to set a date in the New Year. Gorton's run had begun in earnest. They were unanimous though that whoever was to become prime minister, it would be the Liberal Party that would decide. The Country Party would not be voting no matter what the Governor-General had said.

At the same time the campaign to keep McEwen in the top job had begun; independent Tasmanian Senator Reg Turnbull took to the press extolling that *"It is now nationally recognised, except in the Parliamentary Liberal Party, that John McEwen is the man for the job".*[157] National headlines also swung wildly between imploring readers to *"Keep McEwen as PM"* to *'Lib accuses McEwen of treachery"*.[158] The competing views within Australia and who should lead it were being promoted by leading media magnates Rupert Murdoch and Frank Packer mastheads.

There is conjecture about how involved McEwen himself was in this ground campaign for his own candidature. Certainly, he was up to his armpits in maneuvering to block McMahon and promote Gorton, but evidence as to whether this was linked to a broader plan to create a space for himself to be the fallback option is thin and would have been kept very tight in any case. There are however several examples of McEwen 'keeping the gate open' so he could be 'drafted' either by public opinion or by the failure and complexity of the Liberal party processes. The lack of depth within Liberal Party ranks given the Holt disappearance occurred so early in his leadership meant that the party was not up to the rigour this challenge. This was a political party whose identity had centered in one leader ... Menzies. What is certain, though, was that McEwen was in control and using all his acumen, contacts and experience accumulated over 30 years at the pinnacle of national and international politics to secure his desired outcome.

As McEwen was now the Prime Minister alterations to his

farm in Victoria were now needed for security reasons. Local resident Frank Stephens recalls that bitumen road was laid on McEwen land to the driveway of *Chilgala*; from then on the beloved black Buick would not get muddy. A secure phone line was presumably installed (Telstra did not even know this line existed until recently!) — *Chilgala* more than 60 years later still holds so many secrets.

The 20th of December

'Black Jack' McEwen's 25-member ministry was sworn in the following day, without change to its members. In his press conferences that followed, Prime Minister McEwen spoke deliberately of "my ministers", of "my government" and "my cabinet".[159] There is no doubt, this was the McEwen Government. No more acting PM. McEwen, Round 2.

The first pressing task for the new Prime Minister McEwen was to oversee the memorial service for Harold Holt that was to take place in two days. Australia's coming of age as an independent, sovereign nation that understood its geographic location as a strategic and economic regional power had begun with McEwen's trade initiatives and was continued by Holt during his tenure as Prime Minister. McEwen was determined as Prime Minister to demonstrate to the Australian people the respect Australia was held in, internationally. As usual he hit the phones.

The memorial service eventually became an unprecedented gathering of world leaders on home soil, providing a unique opportunity for McEwen's ministers to meet with compatriots face-to-face. His press conferences and public comments were forward leaning with respect to incoming dignitaries and Australia's foreign policy position:

> *We are at this time deeply involved in world events. We share with our allies in Vietnam the responsibilities and agonies of making certain that aggressive Communism cannot overrun a free people. We are having continuous communication with the British Government about its plans for the extent of their continuing involvement in Asia. My Government will continue to act as a responsible and confirmed members of the international community with a special understanding for the Asian people and their problems. Our involvement in defence matters is entirely related to working with right minded people to bring about a more stable world. We are working with all our energy towards fairer international reading opportunities for all countries.*[160]

McEwen had been working internationally for nearly two decades in the trade portfolio and was recognised as "hard but fair" around negotiation tables as the world worked to construct a trading system whose aim was to increase the standard of living for every man. McEwen had driven a fundamental shift in foreign policy away from Britain towards Asia and was keen for his ministers to capitalise on attending leaders. The US President Johnson was a personal friend of Harold Holt's, and declared he would attend the service, calling in to visit Mrs Holt prior to the funeral. The President quietly shed tears during the service for the man that coined "all the way with LBJ" on his last US trip. In truth, this was not the President's only reason for attending, it was essential that the USA was abreast of the leadership crisis threatening their most significant ally in the Vietnam War.

McEwen reaffirmed Australia's commitment to both the South Vietnamese and United States that under his government there was no change to our focus on Vietnam, Australia would "stay steadfast until a just peace was won". According to reports, McEwen's steady hand and unwavering support for the alliance gave the President confidence. In a declassified Presidential daily brief that included Top Secret information on North Vietnam the Central Intelligence Agency (CIA) notes that:

> *Ambassador Clark had a 15-minute talk with Prime Minister McEwen shortly after President Johnson left Melbourne. Prime Minister McEwen told Ambassador Clark that, while the US and Australia have had excellent relations all along, the President's visit 'cemented our relationship for all time.' The ambassador comments that McEwen could not have been more complimentary. The prime minister also said it was the announcement of the President's visit which had caused others—including specifically the British—to send top-level delegations McEwen is very grateful for this.*[161]

On the morning of the service, chief executives of all six of Australia's war allies — America, South Vietnam, South Korea, the Philippines, New Zealand and Thailand - met for a Vietnam summit meeting in Canberra prior to flying to Melbourne for the service.

Initially, newspaper reports signaled that Britain would perhaps send a senior minister and the Duke of Edinburgh. After LBJ confirmed his attendance, an embarrassed British government sent a top level delegation including Prime Minister Harold Wilson — only the second British PM to visit Australia at that time — as well as Her Majesty's loyal

Opposition leader Conservative Edward Heath, together with a youthful HRH Prince of Wales, Charles Windsor, who would be returning to Australia, representing his mother Queen Elizabeth II as heir.

McEwen's meeting schedule was focused on those nations who were significant trading partners and defence allies. These included heavy hitters President Ferdinand Marcos of the Philippines, PM Singapore, Lee Kwan Yew, Malaysian Deputy PM Abdul Razak Hussein, and the British PM Harold Wilson and the British Opposition Leader Edward Heath — all significant reformers of their respective nations. He also discussed trade and security issues with the Indonesian Foreign Affairs Minister and the Vice-President of Japan's ruling party the Liberal Democratic Party (LDP). McEwen also formally called into Government House to meet with the 19-year-old future king, Prince Charles.

McEwen did not have the warm personal relationship with LBJ that Holt had enjoyed, but the two countries were allies confronting growing domestic unrest in the wake of the Vietnam War. And McEwen took his responsibilities seriously. Rather than staying at his regular Canberra residence Kurrajong Hotel, McEwen decamped to the more modern Rex Hotel where the President was lodging and had several formal and informal interactions. The final conversation between President Johnson and the Prime Minister McEwen took place in Melbourne after a luncheon at Government House, post the memorial service in the presidential Lincoln limousine driving out to Tullamarine Airport. McEwen again reiterated his appreciation for the respect that the President's visit had showed for Australia.

Just 24 hours later on the 23 December, President Johnson was on the ground in Vietnam visiting US troops in Cam Ranh Bay,-privately acknowledging the war was lost but thankful for Australia's strong public support.[162]

During meetings in Canberra with President Johnson, McEwen learned of future changes to the United States approach to improving its own balance of payments that would likely impact Australia's economy, including reduced foreign investment.

On his return to the US, President Johnson announced his goal to bringing the US overseas payments into balance in 1968, specifically this would mean a decrease of 65 per cent in US investment into Australia. The Australian Government perspective on foreign investment was an issue the US paid close attention to, being one of the largest investors. In 1966, a CIA intelligence brief reported that foreign investment was under discussion by cabinet. Then Deputy PM McEwen was cited as holding a more *"nationalistic line towards foreign investment"*, whilst PM Holt *"encourages it"*. The brief concluding that Australia's policy towards foreign investment would be unlikely to change over the next few years.[163] And then McEwen became Prime Minister. This New Year's Day announcement by President Johnson, saw Prime Minister McEwen immediately swing into action again. How could he use this announcement by the President to Australia's advantage despite personally agreeing with the decrease in foreign investment?

On 2 January, the Prime Minister McEwen called holidaying ministers to return to Canberra for both the Cabinet Economic Committee, prior to meeting with US Undersecretary Eugene Rostow of the State for Political

Affairs, and a delegation from the US later that week. He also recalled the foreign affairs sub committees of Cabinet. There were also upcoming talks with the United Kingdom which would concern tying their economy and imports tighter to Europe which would have a significant detrimental impact on Australian agricultural exports.

In the leadup to meeting with the US representative on 5 January , McEwen made it clear that whilst recognising a strong US economy was essential for global economic stability, and as such could understand the need to correct balance of payment issues, this decision by the US would damage Australia. His thinking was that given the high level of US investment capital into the country, Australia should be entitled to special reciprocal assistance. As such, it is likely the US President would have been reminded in a quiet, calculated and determined manner of the support in Vietnam by Prime Minister McEwen. This was in line with the way McEwen had approached countless negotiation he had issues with previously, pragmatically extracting significant benefit for his constituents from decisions that he recognised as beyond his control.

As Davey confirms,[164] following five hours of negotiations with US Undersecretary Rostow it was subsequently announced that Australia would be looked on "sympathetically" in determining the flow of capital from the US. Later, in a letter to subsequent Prime Minister Gorton LBJ confirmed that ways to *"offset"* Australia's commitment in Vietnam had been raised by Prime Minster McEwen earlier in the month. The President then proposed *"that Australia supply the sugar requirements of the United States and other free world forces in South Vietnam"*,[165] with an estimated value of $6.5 million

USD. Prime Minister McEwen's ability and experience in pragmatically obtaining 'offsets' (for farmers as a result of detrimental government policies on tariffs and trade) had served the nation well again. Just as US marines were kept warm during freezing Korean winters with Australian wool, going forward US troops would be exclusively eating Australian sugar whilst in Vietnam.

January 9

The Liberals elected Gorton, as expected, despite a late rally for McMahon. When congratulating the newly elected Liberal leader McEwen asked when Gorton would like him to resign ... *how about 2:30pm?"* [166] came the reply from a buoyant but still Senator Gorton. McEwen was stunned. Gorton wanted no hand over, no advice, no briefings, and membership of the House of Representatives was not required either apparently.

In his final two hours as prime minister, McEwen called a rushed Cabinet meeting. Cabinet being the ultimate decision-making body in the Westminster system, McEwen respected the institution and wanted to ensure they endorsed the *"unfortunate"*[167] precedent that next prime minister would not be a member of parliament for a period of time. The 'gate' was closing but they had one more chance to draft him. He gave his Cabinet a choice, saying *"I do not approve of this but I do not propose to oppose it at all"*.[168] Cabinet offered no dissent; the die was cast. He made the precedent Cabinet's to own. He left the meeting and offered his resignation to the Governor-General shortly thereafter.

Cabinet could have taken another approach – it could

have agreed with Prime Minister McEwen, that it was an unacceptable precedent to set and allow McEwen to continue until the new leader of the Liberal Party had been elected to the House of Representatives. Or was it to give his colleagues a chance to decide it could even be longer?

Despite keeping the 'gate' open to continue in the role, Gorton and McMahon had done a deal and the Liberal Party that dominated Cabinet agreed,[169] as an article in the *Australian Financial Review* makes clear! This explains Gorton's desire to be sworn in whilst still a Senator and for a period of time to serve as prime minister from outside parliament against all precedent of the 68 year old federation. What was the trade off? Was it so that McMahon became the Deputy PM or the acting PM if such an event was to occur again to avoid the threat posed by the Country Party holding the position? Was it the Liberal Party ministers putting aside naked personal ambition to ensure it could not be outflanked again if a similar situation were to ever arise at another time? Even so, McEwen fixed that on his way out the door. And leaving Government House that afternoon setting a precedent of his own, extracting an offset if you will. The first sworn Deputy Prime Minister in Australian history. The role of every subsequent leader of the future National Party in a Coalition government by right from then on.

Menzies desired McEwen to succeed him, large sections of the public, parliament and the press thought he was the man (for they were only men then) for the job. A formidable force of nature, this tall ramrod man. Silent, passionate advocate, devastating debater, progressive patriot, Australians knew he was a fighter and had the nation's best interests at heart.

A protectionist right to the end.

Jeff Hook, 21st December 1967. (Used with Permission)

7

THE NEW McEWENISTS

Context is everything. When this book was first envisioned, COVID-19 was not a thing. My reflections of McEwen's contribution to building our nation were to situate his policies and practices in our nation's development. But are those policies relevant today? Is the party McEwen led still championing the same outcomes? Should it be, or as times change, should we?

Revisionist economists and commentators with their own political agendas have long attempted to minimize McEwen's legacy as outdated protectionism — a failed approach unsuitable for a modern, supposedly diverse economy, as Australia is today. This is simply untrue.

McEwenism is about nation building. This is a vision I share.

McEwen's 'protection for all' at its simplest was an economic expression of egalitarianism. McEwen's contribution and vision for our nation extended beyond simply ensuring farmers, manufacturers and workers were able to make a living. Neither is it true to say Country Party interests were some sectional power play to preference one section of the nation ahead of another. Rather, it was recognition that the national interest is best served with strong, prosperous and populous regions and, as such, are fundamental to the prosperity and security of the nation. Instead of these interests being mutually exclusive, they are simply a subset.

It is also contended that adherence to either a *laissez-faire* or a socialist ideology will deliver for country people and their industries and therefore no need of a separate and unique representation within a pluralist liberal democracy. But these same schools of thought are part of a post-1950 Australian intellectual elitism. McMahon and Whitlam, who began the dismantlement of McEwen's policy framework, were actually more similar to each other in upbringing, life-experience and mindset than either was similar to McEwen. They had opposite ideologies, but both were ideologues, nonetheless. What they both lacked was McEwen's pragmatism, his 'doers disregard for precedent'; his focus on the real world not the textbook when implementing policies.

The development and industrialisation of Australia driven by McEwen and supported by Menzies has been deconstructed and derided over subsequent decades to the point where academics now question the social economic and political contribution that he made.[170] Denigrating McEwen as an 'agrarian socialist' completely misses the point. McEwen was a practitioner not a theorist. He was a leader interested in outcomes and real life, not in an imagined utopia found at either end of the political spectrum.

Indeed, McEwen was not one to trumpet his personal manifesto. However, his vision for Australia, if one were to adopt one for him, would be simply that of a strong, prosperous and independent nation that stood up for itself in the world.

McEwen's personal credo underpinned his political party and the hopes he held for his country.

After World War Two, McEwen knew the nation could no longer rely on Britain, and that Australia had to forge its own way. In his own words McEwen, *"held very firm and clear views"*[171] on Australia's international economic relations. Specifically, Australian trade, the development of primary industry exports, tariffs and protection for secondary industry, immigration and foreign investment were his key areas of policy responsibility over many decades.

In 2020, Australia, after a period of great complacency and illusions about the permanence of the leadership of the United States, has similarly awakened to the weakness in our domestic economy, in our sovereign capacity and to the short-sighted of policies that have resulted in an economy that is without sufficient breadth and depth.

And so these questions are now even more relevant as Australia enters a period of great uncertainty, with unprecedented business dislocation, job losses and debt levels, it is therefore instructive to reflect on the post-

World War Two recovery. The plan developed by the reconstruction committee of Chifley included rural reconstruction, immigration and increasing trade exports, and it was largely adapted and implemented by a Country Party Treasurer Fadden and Trade and Industry Minister McEwen under the prime ministership of Menzies. It was Country Party policies that developed our nascent industrial capacity and also protected us from the risk of insecure goods supply chains that World War Two had exposed; which decoupled from our reliance on a fickle Britain for over 25 percent of our exports. They were implemented with the dawning acknowledgement that we alone should determine our destiny. Now, there is a nagging echo of that moment – once again we have become hyper-aware of over-reliant export partnerships, exposed weaknesses in supply chains for crucial goods and the need to develop a capacity in sectors previously let go. We are suddenly remembering that foreign investment should be in the national interest and that strategic assets need to be protected from opportunistic buyers.

The Country Party was created to overcome the disadvantage of geography. Its mandate was clear, to support policies that support the wealth generating industries, securing jobs for country Australians post World War One. Over subsequent decades its focus remains unchanged. Agriculture, mining and manufacturing are the pillars for its policy focus. Access to quality health care, telecommunications and education in the 21st century also received attention as it became clear that regional Australians outcomes were often worse.

This is not a party built for globalists. Rather, localism is at its very heart. It has a broader constituency than was first envisioned a century ago; now encompassing local small business owners and entrepreneurs in regional centres and country towns, the manufacturers and the miners, the fishers and the foresters.

For John McEwen, principles of full employment meant backing primary and secondary industries domestically. Fighting for an international rules-based trading system that just did not favour the big guys. It was a very National Party approach to a fight – understanding that efficiency was not the only metric to measure success. As Adam Smith argues the dual purpose of a national economy is *"first to provide a plentiful revenue or subsistence for people, or more properly to provide such revenue or subsistence for themselves; and second, to supply the state or commonwealth with a revenue sufficient for public services"*.[172] Full employment and providing the policy settings for small businesses and entrepreneurs to prosper is the task of governments. McEwen agreed and worked tirelessly to that end. For McEwen, having experienced the deprivation, seen the devastation that government policies could wreak on a family and industry, he was determined to do it differently.

Fast-forward to today and the truth is that those precepts and McEwen's approach still hold true for our Party. Moreover, ironically, they have become more universally shared across the political spectrum in the light of recent social and economic shocks brought on by the global Covid19 pandemic.

Apologies to both Smith and Frydenberg, but the invisible hand of McEwen lies behind Australia's Covid-19 recovery response.

At a national level it would seem we are all *McEwenists* now.

A new focus on full employment has been laid out by the Reserve Bank of Australia, which has now raised the bar that the measure of the success of our economic policy settings should be our employment rate.

As a government this is not re-advocating protectionism, but there is a major rethink based on national interest on local manufacturing, protection of our strategic economic assets from predatory overseas companies, of self-sufficiency and ownership in areas such as energy, utility assets, communications and critical minerals, and the need to diversify our trading markets and our product offerings.

Prominent journalists were quick to identify this big policy shift; Paul Kelly coining the phrase 'pandemic protectionism' while Michelle Grattan talked of Morrison's "pandemic pragmatism," but the Morrison Government's sole focus has been to pragmatically "protect" Australian lives and livelihoods, how ever they can.[173]

On the other hand, the essential policy imperatives that were the focus of McEwen are still the front and centre for the Nationals today. Regionalism, decentralisation, employment for all, growing our share of international trade to build our common wealth, securing and defending our borders and our way of life, maintaining our independence as a sovereign nation, are among our shared values. Given the diversity of Nationals MPs these core issues are also pragmatically understood through the lens of localism.

Because we come from Australian country towns and cities the National Party has a practical approach to solving these policy questions. For the National Party, as the second party of government, it is through the judicious accrual and careful use of political power that outcomes are achieved. McEwen's approach highlights his commitment to strong stable government, robust informed policy decisions and a fearlessness to unashamedly put regional Australians first - the ultimate specialist. Power is held, force is its use. McEwen forced his hand with his coalition partners only twice; the rest of his significant achievements were won as a result of holding institutional authority, being across the detail, using a range of methods, from standover tactics to compassionate supplication and importantly leading a team galvanised by their collective unity of purpose. These were Country Party MPs that didn't forget where they came from, who it was who had sent them to Canberra, and what their job was whilst they had the privilege to represent their people.

Today's Nationals should not confuse the need for steely resolve, clarity of purpose and an ability to argue the detail with flaccid acquiescence nor immature tantrums as a means of achieving outcomes for our people. McEwen and his party won through, because the case was calmly made that the national interest was best served when regional industries, people and the party that represented them were respected and considered. Delivering for country Australia can sometimes mean extracting concessions in the face of government decisions that negatively impact regional interest or indeed using ministerial discretion to deliver grant programs that provide for local priorities to be realised. But the ultimate goal should be policy grounded in the principles such as 'country mindedness', egalitarianism, protection of property rights and national sovereignty.

To understand the Nationals, one also needs to understand

how its cultural background intersects with politics. We are proud of who we are and where we come from – we do things a little differently out there. We are proud of our nation, its contribution to the world – a generation of light horsemen is remembered every year, in every town a century later. We are proud of our heritage, our families, our footy teams and our towns. We are proud of our pastimes - water-skiing on the Murray, hunting in the great outdoors, our array of sports and local theatre, poets and storytelling. We volunteer for everything. Our people ask: What is wrong with being a patriot? What is wrong with wanting to protect your family, your business, your way of life, your values or your nation? Nothing. The lived localism of the regions taps the deepest of human needs – to connect, to each other and the natural environment. Because after all, all politics is local. Politics is about people.

Security

> *"It would have been ridiculous to think Australia was safe in the long term unless we built up our population and built up our industries."*[174]

In his autobiography McEwen raised clear concerns he had about post-World War Two Australia having a large land mass without the critical population base required to defend against an invasion, and that the influx of immigrants needed work to be able to provide for their families and contribute to their new country.

Today, there are different concerns about population policy. Without a strong immigration program, a smaller and older Australia awaits us. The policy emphasis is on attracting skilled and business migrants; people ready to work hard to contribute to our national story. Strong economic growth has been propped up by increases in population through immigration. As Greg Sheridan stated recently, *"the chief security damage of the virus is that it cuts our population growth. We should address that as a priority"*.[175] With immigration abruptly halted other drivers such as investment in innovation and technology; industrial relations reform centred on productivity improvements are now essential.

As Nationals, we do not advocate for population growth as an end in itself. We also want a population that is more evenly distributed across the country in order to provide opportunities for people to live and settle in regional towns and cities and to enjoy the way of life we love. In a period where the large cities have left young people out of the housing market, the regions still offer that Australian dream.[176] But there must also be the opportunities for work, for educational advancement and to equality in health care and other government services taken for granted in the cities.

Prosperity

Supporting primary industries, expanding secondary industry to create jobs.

McEwen backed wealth generating industries, primarily mining, agriculture, and manufacturing as a secondary industry. Seeking to protect a nascent industry as our competitors had done, exposing them to competition over time. He did not support propping up inefficient industries, knowing that some could 'grow fat' behind tariff walls; but he also believed that *"it is also necessary to take account of things beside efficiency. There was one constant though in my mind: we had a workforce to employ".*[177]

Today this remains true, increasing the value of products exported by value-adding here at home whether in food, fibre or in engineering firms. Covid 19 has exposed two critical issues for Australia — our decreased manufacturing capability and our over-reliance on fragile global supply chains to source critical goods. Regional Australia already manufactures over 30 percent of our current product range, and this is set to increase. We need to ensure that regional Australia is the focus for investment by backing existing players to grow, and in new advanced manufacturing plants and capability.

Regional manufacturing faces huge challenges including a fragmented approach to regional development, rising energy costs, access to a skilled workforce, failure to invest in research and development into new technologies and processes, connecting infrastructure of transport and communication, and water security to name a few. This means strategic support for existing national areas of strength, rather than 'picking winners'. Yet the regions can be used to harness existing population trends that back movement away from cities and look to localise manufacturing supply chains.

Expanding export offerings and markets

I am a free trader, but like McEwen a pragmatic one. I am not an advocate for returning to a protectionist tariff and quota system as this would not be in our national interest. Australia depends on trade, one in every five jobs is as a result of our status as a trading nation. We should be expanding both our markets and suite of products on offer, but not if it requires Australia to sacrifice our local interest for an imagined globalist trading agenda.

And now more than ever we must be focused on trade, expanding our markets (as McEwen did when he was at his best), promoting our products, and value-adding to our products. But we need to recalibrate our focus. The Department of Trade should be separated from its big sister. We need a trader's focus on trade, not a diplomat's focus on trade. So, their one focus isn't playing nice in the sandpit, it is about achieving outcomes, and driving hard bargains at the negotiating table.

The pragmatic reality is that refined intellect rarely shakes the grimy hand of commerce. Indeed, it has been argued that merging foreign affairs and trade is like featuring artichokes in a bouquet of roses.

Foreign policy is crafted by diplomats, bureaucrats, and politicians in a remote Canberra conclave, while trade is driven by forces remote from Canberra — in our capitals and regions — and by distant market needs, rather than central policy dictates. Our trade architecture must reflect that difference. Trade must now regain its place in the pantheon of much needed economic reforms, as we strive to supercharge our economic recovery.

We must also recognise that trade is just one side of our economic coin. If we are to reduce supply chain dependence on other nations, and become more self-reliant, re-build manufacturing, and encourage further processing, then trade and investment must join hands with industry and innovation policy, with a common, parallel agenda.

Sovereignty

As a patriot, the national interest was always at the forefront of McEwen's thinking, he often commented with respect to foreign investment in agricultural assets that Australia was *"selling the farm one piece at a time"*. He was cautious of foreign investment, and approached trading negotiations prepared to walk away if he could not secure an adequate deal. His engagement with the post-war world was serious and engaged, shaping international frameworks in our young national interest, building coalitions where he could and extracting offsets in the face of potential defeat. His approach to defence and population policy also highlighted the importance he placed on ensuring the unique perspective and position of Australia's interests were prosecuted. This often put him in conflict with his senior coalition partner.

The Nationals have long championed stronger oversight of foreign investment, particularly land and water and agribusinesses, but recognising the necessary tensions between critical capital investment in manufacturing, mining and agriculture assets and maintenance of local control. As the globe retreats to parochialism, the Nationals must ride the problematic relationship between investment, trading opportunities and maintaining our national independence.

McEwen's idea of freedom to be 'one's own boss' is still a core principle for farmers and small businesses alike. Who controls critical wealth producing industries is not an academic question simply because 'they can't take it with them'. It is a question of control, of commitment to our shared prosperous future, not in some faraway place but here, locally. Similarly, Australia should seek to build coalitions with other liberal democratic trading nations to ensure that the global trading framework we operate in reflects the reality that 58 percent of world trade is now conducted with controlled economies. Hardly a free globalised trade environment envisioned by the original architects.

Conclusion

After his retirement from politics McEwen continued to show optimism for his country.[178]

Australia is now living in a period of great uncertainty - typically our economic and strategic interests have been cohesive. They are now incongruent. A trade war between our strategic ally and our economic partner threatens our national interest like never before. A global pandemic has collided into an untested, immature federation causing a domestic crisis of our own making.

The principles of *McEwenism* and the policies he chose to implement were not popular in and of themselves. They were subsequently popular, because Australians were proud of standing on their own two feet, and because the wealth created set Australia up for a long period of prosperity. McEwen's policies articulated a modern version of a nation which had come of age in a Second World War, prepared to compete with the world whether on agricultural commodities or at the 1956 Melbourne Olympics. These policies articulated our identity, as a modern, fledgling, first world industrialised nation, secure, sovereign and prosperous. Now, out of global uncertainty and necessity, we are obliged as patriots to McEwen's principles.

To this extent we owe a deep debt of gratitude to this great

Australian man.

A country man.

A pragmatic patriot.

APPENDIX 1

National Party Leaders on McEwen

McEwen's impact on the Country Party was immense, the leaders who followed him reflect on his contribution.

Doug Anthony 2 February 1971 - 17 January 1984

McEwen was a strong man. He was at times a hard, tough and demanding man. He had a commanding presence, a personality of great force. He was a man of integrity and a man of honour. He was a powerful negotiator. He was a persuasive advocate. He knew how to put his views and to win his arguments.

McEwen was the best politician from any party I have ever seen. He was shrewd. He never showed any fear. He liked to attack people, but he had great political wit … He was the best of all politicians as far as strategy is concerned.

John McEwen was not just a politician or a political leader, but a statesman. He looked like a statesman. He behaved like a statesman. He spoke like a statesman. He had a statesman's bearing. He was a statesman. Above all, he was an Australian, and Australia was the better for his presence.

Ian Sinclair 17 January 1984 – 9 May 1989

McEwen had one very effective capability; he normally chose to speak last. His timing of intervention of debating was impeccable and effective.

McEwen was very effective in debate normally choosing to speak last. His timing of intervention was impeccable. He would summarise previous argument, identify his opposition or support and then state his case. Doug Anthony, Peter Nixon and I were very fortunate to have served in successive Cabinets under his leadership.

Charles Blunt 9 May 1989 – 6 April 1990

It is a great pity, that McEwen, dour and private, reserved and not given to sharing thoughts and inner feelings, did not leave more insights into his thinking and motives. His biography is matter of fact, more factual than opinion. We would be richer with more clues into his motives, hopes and aspirations. Even an insight into his dreams for the future. Known as 'Black Jack' or as Menzies called him 'Le Noir' many see McEwen in monochrome. While by todays ephemeral colorful and undisciplined social media driven political scene, McEwen looks pale grey he really was more than one dimensional. He was often a formidable battleship grey, especially at the Dispatch Box, a threatening black on the wrong side of an argument or a persuasive silver light when chasing a goal or objective.

Interestingly, after a generation free open trade, open markets, expansive, multi-national company led globalization, politics worldwide is seeing the emergence of middle class resistance of the global model and its costs to local industry, the price paid by local communities and workers through distortion and supply chain short weaknesses. The reassessment driven by community actions, has been picked up at government level in many countries. McEwen would recognize the politics of this reassessment. If McEwen were a participant on the political process today, he would be different, with different priorities but priorities that he saw as important to constituency. Would he succeed? In touch with his voters; yes I think he would resonate and succeed. I cannot imagine him performing stunts for a photo opportunity, but he would be happy to wear a day-glow vest to mix with workers, he would never be called a Political Poodle. 'Black Jack' would always have the bearing of a Big Dog, a no frills, uniquely Australian working dog.

In a political party of fabled Leaders, McEwen stands out. Made by his personal experiences, underestimated by many, driven by an ambition to achieve and succeed he achieved enduring influence and created a political legend.

Tim Fischer 10 April 1990 – 1 July 1999

It is time we corrected the continual rewriting of history including war time history by Labor. They talk of the McEwen years in terms of a backward-looking nation. It is a lie of huge proportions. So, let me highlight four McEwen actions which help facilitate a fair assessment of Sir Jack McEwen and his place in history.

Firstly, it was Jack McEwen who gave direction to this nation's migration policy in 1938 by opening up migration from Holland and laying down guidelines used by subsequent Labor Ministers for Immigration.

Secondly, it was McEwen in 1940 who, as Minister for External Affairs, appointed ambassadors to countries outside the British Empire for the first time, totally destroying the Keating thesis we never thought beyond Britain.

Thirdly, it was McEwen in 1957 who forced through – against considerable opposition – the first trade treaty to be signed between Australia and Japan, in turn leading to Japan becoming Australia's largest trading partner. This was opposed by Labor at the time but has given a huge boost to Australia over the years, including beef and sugar.

Fourthly, it was Jack McEwen who in 1961 moved to abolish all import licences totally and dramatically reduced the exceptionally high level of export protection which had been adding to the cost of Australian industry.

John Anderson 1 July1999 – 23 June 2005

He was a very, very impressive individual, quite driven and a clear thinker. He certainly had Menzies' respect. McEwen as essentially a very pragmatic man. A man who saw well into the future though. Most people who can see into the future are actually people who had understood the past. As Churchill said, "all you want to know of statecraft can be learnt by studying history". I suspect Menzies and McEwen had a brilliant partnership. The Australian people have to perceive that you are doing it for sound reasons. Not yourself. And I think that was a great part of McEwen's success. The Country Party were essentially free traders, so I think the kind of interpretation of McEwen's position was that he thought if he couldn't get rid of tariffs he darn well made sure that they worked to the benefit of country people.

Appendix

Mark Vaile 23 June 2005 – 3 December 2007

The relationship between Australia and Japan is a very historic one going back to the fifties when Black Jack McEwen signed the commerce agreement with Japan in 1957. In 2003 the relationship was enhanced further when Prime Minister Howard and Prime Minister Koizumi signed a trade and economic framework. That laid down a new set of guidelines in terms of the way trade is done between the two countries.

The economic relationship between Australia and Japan is a long and historic one going back to the 1950's when 'Black Jack' McEwen signed the Commerce Agreement with Japan in 1957. This stood as the foundation of the relationship through to 2003. Continuing to build on the 1957 Agreement, Prime Ministers Howard and Koizumi signed the Australia-Japan Trade and Economic Framework. Then in 2015, to build a closer relationship, Prime Ministers Abbott and Abe signed the Japan-Australia Economic Partnership Agreement. That laid down a new set of guidelines in terms of the way trade is done between the two countries. Today almost 80 per cent of Australian exports to Japan enter duty free and 87 per cent have duties of less than 10 per cent.

It is incumbent upon us to recognise that the strong trading relationship we have with Japan started many decades ago. It was actually instigated over 60 years ago by 'Black Jack' McEwen, who identified how important the rise and industrialisation of Japan would be to Australia's economic future.

We should recognise that this coalition government, now in its fourth term, has continued delivering Australian exporters extra access into this very important market.

Warren Truss 7 December 2005 – 11 February 2016

Although I did not have the good fortune to meet 'Black Jack', I share his farming background and his passion for a fair go for regional Australia. Sir John McEwen was arguably the greatest of The National Party's leaders.

He was a champion of the farming community and travelled extensively throughout regional Australia and the outback. In his early career in the ministry, he worked hard to bring primary industry leaders into closer contact with government. The wool, wheat and meat industry in particular, owe a great deal to his determination to secure a better deal for farmers. It was an era when these commodities made up two thirds of our nation's export income. But he was also a great advocate for manufacturing in this country especially processing our agricultural produce and natural resources. Although the arguments and controversy over protectionism were to dog the last years of his long political career, he left a lasting legacy in improving the administration of Australia's primary industry, and the decisive shaping of international trade politics in the crucial 1950's and early 1960's.

'Black Jack' was a visionary with a great love of his country. Perhaps his greatest achievement was negotiating a groundbreaking Commerce Agreement with Japan. This must have been an heroic and far-sighted achievement for a soldier settler just a decade after the end of World War Two. This Agreement led to a major expansion of Australia's trade and still forms the basis of the modern Free Trade Agreements we have with Japan and many other nations around the world.

Sir John will always be remembered as one of Australia's

great political gladiators and a champion of Australian industry and the Nationals.

Barnaby Joyce 12 February 2016 – 26 February 2018

So why John 'Black Jack' McEwen? Hair combed back with Brylcream, jutting square jaw, dark ominous eyebrows, a man who had worked with his own hands on the land. He was not Oxbridge but was paddock shrewd from a tougher life. He personified the way so many from the country saw their relationship with power in Canberra. Respect and never believe we owe you our support. You will never be the government without the vote away from the capitals.

McEwen was the steel in that leadership partnership with Menzies. He remains the gold standard we mark the leaders of the National Party against. We could talk of policy but it's his leadership that fascinates me. No Billy you can't be prime minister! Robert if this doesn't happen the government falls. They followed him and we still follow him now.

Michael McCormack 26 February 2018-

Formidable yet compassionate – Sir John McEwen was both and so much more. Known and respected far and wide as 'Black Jack', this giant of Australian politics served our nation – particularly those in country areas – mightily. He was visionary in trade, determined to see regional Australians get the services they deserve and always a man of the people. He never, ever forgot his first duty of care – rural and regional Australians. Bold, forthright, humble and caring –

all attributes of McEwen's makeup. He ranks amongst the best in the pantheon of prime ministers and Country and National Party leaders who have proudly and magnificently occupied a seat of power in our nation's government.

APPENDIX 2

JOHN McEWEN: 29 March 1900 – 20 November 1980

Career Record & Honours

Parliamentary career:

15/09/1934 – 23/10/1937 Federal Member for Echuca, Victoria

23/10/1937 – 10/12/1949 Federal Member for Indi, Victoria 29/11/1937 – 26/04/1939 Minister for Interior

14/03/1940 – 28/10/1940 Minister for External Affairs

27/10/1940 – 03/10/1941 Member Australian War Cabinet

28/10/1940 – 07/10/1941 Minister for Air & Civil Aviation

16/10/1941 – 31/081945 Member Australian Advisory War Council

22/09/1943 – 26/03/1958 Deputy Leader, Australian Country Party

10/12/1949 – 01/02/1971 Federal Member for Murray, Victoria (resigned position)

19/12/1949 – 11/01/1956 Minister for Commerce & Agriculture

11/01/1956 – 18/12/1963 Minister for Trade

12/1958 – 02/1971 Acting Prime Minister 24 occasions totalling 550 days between

26/03/1958 – 19/12/1967 Deputy Prime Minister

26/03/1958 – 01/02/1971 Leader, Australian Country Party

18/12/1963 – 05/02/1971 Minister for Trade & Industry

19/12/1967 – 10/01/1968 Prime Minister

Honours:

1st June 1953 Appointed to the Queen's Privy Council, PC Order of the Companion of Honour, CH,

1st January 1969 For services as Deputy Prime Minister of Australia

1st January 1971 Order of Saint Michael & Saint George Knight Grand Cross, GCMG, for services to the Commonwealth

5 February 1973 Order of the Rising Sun First Class (Japan), in recognition of furthering friendly relations between Australia & Japan

ENDNOTES

1. Malcolm Fraser in John Howard *The Menzies Era - The Years that Shaped Modern Australia*, Harper Collins Publishers, Sydney, 2014, pp. 236-7.
2. John McEwen, *John McEwen: His Story*, 2nd edn, Page Research Centre, Canberra, 2014, p. 48.
3. Malcolm Fraser in Peter Golding, *Black Jack McEwen-Political Gladiator*, Melbourne University Press, Carlton, 1996, p. 192.
4. McEwen, *John McEwen: His Story*, p. 37.
5. Paul Kelly, "Economic Reform: A Lost Cause or merely in Eclipse?" Inaugural Alf Rattigan Lecture, 7 December 2016, p. 2 (Kelly quotes Prime Minister Gough Whitlam's 1974 speech to the Heavy Equipment Manufacturers' Association dinner).
6. Andrew Black, Conversation with author, June 2020.
7. Kelly, 'Economic Reform,' p. 3.
8. Peter Nixon, Conversation with author, June 2020.
9. John Crawford, in *John McEwen: His Story*, p. iv.
10. Colin Teese, "The Achievement of John McEwen," *Quadrant*, November, Vol 41, 1997, p. 69.
11. John McEwen, Speech to the Australian Club in London, 17 April 1962.
12. "*...the objective of maximum freedom in trade and other matters which we believe.*" John McEwen, Hansard, 1966, pp. 44-5.
13. McEwen, *John McEwen: His Story*, p. 52.
14. John McEwen, *Ministerial Statement: Australia and the European Common Market*, presented House of Representatives, 3 May 1962.
15. Nixon, Conversation with author, June 2020.
16. Dr Kym Anderson, Conversation with author, June 2020.
17. "*Protection from import competition was a defining feature of the birth of the Australian federation in 1901. For the next 70s years, the extent of protection grew, and broadened from mainly tariffs to also involving import licensing after World War II... Australia*

was the world's most protected advanced economy apart from New Zealand."- see Kym Anderson, "Trade Protectionism in Australia: Its Growth and Dismantling," Centre for Economic Policy Research, *Discussion Paper*, No. DP14760. 2020, p. 1.

18. John W Howard, Conversation with author, July 2020.
19. Gerard Henderson, *Menzies' Child : The Liberal Party of Australia, 1944-1994*, Allen & Unwin, St Leonards, 1994, pp. 36-7.
20. Howard, Conversation with author, July 2020.
21. John Fuller, in Golding, *Black Jack McEwen*, p. 189.
22. Paul Keating, MP, "Death of John McEwen Speech," CPD, HR, 25 November 1980, pp. 33-34.
23. McEwen, (1952), in Golding, *Black Jack McEwen*. p. 45.
24. Ibid., pp. 166-7.
25. Nixon, Conversation with author, June 2020.
26. Pat McNamara, Conversation with author, June 2020.
27. See John Crawford, *The Development of Trade Policy*, University of Western Australia Press, Nedlands, Perth, 1968.
28. McEwen, *John McEwen: His Story*, p. 60.
29. Crawford, *The Development of Trade Policy*.
30. Nixon, Conversation with the author, 2020.
31. John Stone, Conversation with the author, 2020.
32. Maximillian Walsh, *Poor Little Rich Country: A Political History of the 1970s*, Penguin Books, Ringwood,1979, p. 37.
33. Golding, *Black Jack McEwen*, author's discussion with Westerman, p. 328.
34. Ibid.
35. Peter Drysdale, Conversation with author, June 2020.
36. John Anderson, Conversation with author, June 2020.
37. Alf Rattigan, *Industry Assistance: The Inside Story*, Melbourne University Press, Carlton, 1986, pp. 7-8.
38. Ibid., p.10.
39. Golding, *Black Jack McEwen*, p. 326.
40. Anderson, Conversation with author, June 2020.
41. *The Age*, 26 January 1971, p.9.

42. Nigel McCarthy, "Alf Rattigan and the journalists; advocacy journalism and agenda setting in the Australian tariff debate 1963-1971," *Australian Journalism Review*, Vol 22, No 2, 2000, pp. 88-102.
43. *Sydney Morning Herald*, 28 January 1971.
44. Golding, *Black Jack McEwen*, p. 330.
45. Paul Kelly, "Black Jack: Is he Godfather of the Banana Republic?" *Weekend Australian*, 26-27 July 1986.
46. Don Aitkin, 1952 cited in Rae Wear, "Country-mindedness and the Nationals," in Linda Courtenay Botterill, and Geoff Cockfield, (eds), *The National Party- Prospects for the Great Survivors*, Page Research Centre, Allen & Unwin, St Leonards, 2009, p. 82.
47. Ibid.
48. McEwen, *John McEwen His Story*, p. 1.
49. *Federal Standard*, (Chiltern), 4 October 1907.
50. McEwen, *John McEwen: His Story*, p. 2.
51. Ibid.
52. Ibid.
53. Ibid., p. 3.
54. Ibid., p. 5.
55. Lady Ann McEwen, "New man in the PM chair," *Australian Women's Weekly*, 20 May, 1959.
56. According to Stanhope local, Murray Buzza, in conversation with author June 2020.
57. Frank Stephens, Conversation with author, June 2020.
58. Murray Buzza, Conversation with author, June 2020.
59. Bruce D. Graham, *The Formation of the Australian Country Parties*, Australian National University Press, Canberra, 1965, p. 51.
60. Bob Holschiver, viewed 17 July 2020, accessed from soldier-settlement.porv.vic.gov.au/soldiers-stories/john-mcewen/
61. Robert Menzies, in Golding, *Black Jack McEwen*, p. 47.
62. Graham, *The Formation of the Australian Country Parties*, p. xx.
63. Ibid., p. 15.
64. *"Every class but the farmer has been organised for years, and he is*

paying the piper for not being so. The manufacturers get their duties increased, labourers get wage increased and hours shortened, and businessmen pass the increased prices on. The farmers can't pass it on, and to make matters worse, when a natural shortage comes and prices go up, city interests fix the price to suit themselves, and the farmers just have to take it: and so this will continue until we do as the labouring men did. The city wants a city man to represent it - he understands its wants and needs. The country likewise should have a country man represent it, and who understands the wants of the country better than the farmers. Therefore, it behoves every farmer to cast a class-conscious vote for the farmers' representative" - Tongala Branch Victoria Farmers Unions (the Victorian Country Party), October 1917 in Ibid., pp. 43-4.

65. McNamara, Conversation with author, June 2020.
66. Graham, *The Formation of the Australian Country Parties*, p. 68.
67. Country Party historian Andrew Black has recently noted in an unpublished thesis that Dunstan's Country-Labor partnership is an example of a phenomenon throughout the western world of the co-operation of farmers and urban socialists during the interwar period, particularly prevalent during the Depression. He has identified parallel 'Green-Red' partnerships in Canada and Scandinavia at this time.
68. Nixon, Conversation with author, June 2020.
69. Golding, *Black Jack McEwen*, p. xxii.
70. McEwen, *John McEwen: His Story*, p. 31.
71. Bruce Lloyd, Conversation with the author, June 2020.
72. McEwen, *John McEwen: His Story*, p. 9.
73. Paul Kelly, *The End of Certainty- Power, Politics and Business in Australia*, (2nd edn), Allen & Unwin, St Leonards, 1994, p. 6.
74. McEwen, *John McEwen: His Story*, pp. 84-5.
75. John McEwen, CPD, HR, 30 October 1970, p. 3152.
76. Heather Radi, "Stanley Melbourne Bruce," in *Dictionary of Australian Biography: 1891-1939, Volume*, p. 460.
77. According to Golding, *Black Jack McEwen*, p. 167.
78. McEwen, *John McEwen: His Story*, p.29.
79. Ibid., p.31.

80. Ibid.
81. John Crawford, in McEwen, *John McEwen: His Story*, p. iv.
82. McEwen, *John McEwen: His Story*, p. 47.
83. Ibid.
84. John Crawford, in McEwen, *John McEwen: His Story*, p. iv.
85. McEwen, *John McEwen: His Story*, p. 18.
86. Ibid., p. 19.
87. Ibid., p. 27.
88. 'Commonwealth Government to Lord Caldecote, UK Secretary of State for Dominion Affairs (Cablegram 303)', 1940 (18 June) No 400, in H. Kenway, H.J.W. Stokes, P.G. Edwards, *Documents on Australian Foreign Policy: 1937-49*, Volume III: January-June 1940; Volume IV: July 1940-June 1941), 1979.
89. Georges Pelcier, Governor of New Caledonia, to R.G. Menzies, 26 June, 1940 No:439, in Ibid.
90. See McEwen *John McEwen: His Story*, p. 22: "I decided we must try to replace the government with one that was pro-de Gaulle."
91. Departmental Memorandum to J. McEwen, 1940. No: 440, Kenway, et al, *Documents on Australian Foreign Policy: 1937-49*.
92. Stanley Bruce also suggested this to Menzies in a cablegram received on 26 June; see S. M. Bruce, to R.G. Menzies, 1940. (no.438) in Kenway, et al, *Documents on Australian Foreign Policy: 1937-49*.
93. See McEwen, *John McEwen:His Story*, p. 22.
94. "Instructions drafted by Department of External Affairs for Mr B.C. Ballard, Official Representative in New Caledonia," (c August 1940), in Kenway, et al, *Documents on Australian Foreign Policy: 1937-49*.
95. B.C.Ballard,1940 (30 August) No. 85, in Ibid.
96. *Sunday Telegraph*, 6 May 1962, p.7.
97. John Lawrey wrote extensively about this episode in his book *The Cross of the Lorraine in the South Pacific*, but does not credit McEwen as one of the operation's masterminds and postulates that he may have been an opponent to it. It is true that the cablegram records do not explicitly show McEwen as the puppet master he claims to have been (except War Cabinet Minute 498;

114. of *op cit*.), and much of the impetus appears to stem from Sir Harry Luke. However, McEwen is not one to embellish his own record. This was a favourite story of McEwen's and there is no record of repudiation of McEwen's role as a chief author of the coup by its other key players such as Menzies, Luke, Ballard, Captain Showers, or de Gaulle.

98. "General Charles de Gaulle last month recalled a one-man revolution in the Pacific that changed the course of World War II" in *Sunday Telegraph*, 6 May1962, p. 7.
99. (Courage, more courage and ever more courage) Originally said by French Revolutionary Georges Danton and reportedly quoted by Churchill's assistant Morton, when UK Department of External Affairs secretary A.T. Sterling sought clarification on the New Caledonia plan
100. McEwen, *John McEwen: His Story*, pp. 85-86.
101. Nixon, Conversation with author, June 2020.
102. Alan Reid, *The Power Struggle*, Tartan Press, Sydney, 1972, p.19.
103. Peter Robinson, cited in Golding, *Black Jack McEwen*, p. 196.
104. A reference to the devil Mephistopheles from German legend, synonymous with cunning, slyness, wickedness, or ruthless intelligence.
105. Ian Sinclair, CPD, HR, 25 November 1980, pp. 34-35. (speeches made in Parliament on the passing of Sir John McEwen).
106. See further Golding, *Black Jack McEwen*, pp. 29-31.
107. McEwen, *John McEwen: His Story*, p. 65.
108. Bill Baxter, Conversation with author, June 2020.
109. McEwen, *John McEwen:His Story*, p. 77.
110. Crawford, in McEwen, *John McEwen: His Story*, p. iii.
111. Golding, *Black Jack McEwen*, p. 26.
112. McEwen, *John McEwen:His Story,* p. 74.
113. Larry Anthony, Conversation with author, June 2020.
114. Nixon, Conversation with author, June 2020.
115. Ian Sinclair, Conversation with author, June 2020.
116. Nixon, Conversation with author, June 2020.

117. Doug Anthony, in Golding, *Black Jack McEwen*, p. viii.
118. McEwen passed away on the 20th of November 1980 in Toorak, Victoria, from Anorexia metabolic failure weeks and nutritional failure for years. Birth Certificate 27942/80.
119. Sinclair, CPD, HR, 25 November 1980, pp. 34-35
120. Special Correspondent, "McEwen--Strength Through Growth," *The Australian*, 4 January 1968.
121. Kelly, "Economic Reform," p. 5.
122. Ibid.
123. Ibid.
124. Peter Nixon, *An Active Journey: The Peter Nixon Story*, Connor Court Publishing, Ballarat, 2012, p. 92.
125. David Speers, quoting Don Chipp, Sky News 7 April 2019 accessed 15/07/2020.
126. For full account of this letter see: William Hudson, *Casey*, Oxford University Press, Melbourne, 1986, pp. 306-8.
127. Ibid.
128. William McMahon, Correspondence to Prime Minister Holt, 11 December 1967, in Prime Minister's Official papers contained in his briefcase at the time of his disappearance 17 December 1067, National Archives of Australia (NAA): M1945,1, pp. 28-30.
129. Ibid.
130. Peter Lawler, cited in Golding, *Black Jack McEwen*, pp. 267-8.
131. John McEwen, 'Press Statement', 17 December 1967, cited Paul Davey *The Country Party Prime Ministers-Their Trials and Tribulations*, Museum of Australian Democracy, Canberra, 2011, p. 94.
132. Sinclair, Conversation with author, June 2020.
133. Nixon, Conversation with author, June 2020.
134. Howard, *The Menzies Era*, p. 508.
135. McEwen, *John McEwen: His Story*, p. 90.
136. Ibid.
137. Nixon, Conversation with author, June 2020.
138. Ibid.
139. McEwen, *John McEwen: His Story*, p. 69.
140. Ibid.

141. Ibid., p. 67.
142. Sarah Newton, *Maxwell Newton: No Ordinary Man*, Fremantle Arts Centre Press, Fremantle,1993, pp. 11-12.
143. Ibid., p. 163.
144. Clyde Packer, *No Return Ticket*, Angus & Robertson, North Ryde, 1984, p. 118.
145. "Top Secret Personal Memo, Maxwell Newton," 20 October 1967, NAA: M4298, 2, pp. 40-1.
146. "A confidential letter to Prime Minister Holt," 9 November 1968, responding to direct questions, NAA: M4298, 2, p. 45.
147. Stone, Conversation with author, June 2020.
148. Ibid.
149. Ibid.
150. "I told the Prime Minister that on the afternoon of his swearing in as prime minister, Mr. McEwen had asked me to visit him. I did so and had a discussion with him that evening. He asked me whether I had material of security significance on Maxwell Newton. I had replied that I had, in that I had received a report from REDACTED to the effect that this man had removed without authority several documents from a table during the conference of Commonwealth Finance Ministers which had been held in Jamaica…" Notes of Discussion: Prime Minister, Senator J.G. Gorton/Director-General of Security, on Thursday, 1 February, 1968, Melbourne, in NAA: A6119,2544, p. 85.
151. *The Australian*, "The wrong man will be chosen," 8 January 1968.
152. See Bruce Page, *The Murdoch Archipelago*, Simon & Schuster Australia, Sydney, 2011.
153. "Maxwell Newton – Spoiling Operations," NAA: A6119, 2544.
154. Ibid., p. 87.
155. Ibid.
156. Richard Casey, 18 December 1968, "Press Release," cited in Davey, *The Country Party Prime Ministers*, p. 1, 4.
157. "Senator calls for McEwen to stay as PM," *The Australian*, January 1968.
158. "Lib accuses McEwen of treachery," *Sydney Morning Herald*, 9

January 1968.
159. See "The new PM reports to the nation," *Canberra Times*, 20 December 1968
160. Ibid.
161. Criminal Intelligence Agency, *The President's Daily Brief*, 23 December1967.
162. See Influential Presidential Visits' in RealClearPolitics, Accessed 27/07/2020 from: https://www.realclearpolitics.com/lists/influential_presidential_visits/lyndon_johnson_vietnam.html.
163. Central Intelligence Agency, 'President's daily brief,' (11 October) 1966.
164. See Davey, *The Country Party Prime Ministers,* p. 115.
165. Lyndon B. Johnson, "Australia's Contribution to the Allied Cause in Vietnam," received by John G. Gorton, Prime Minister of Australia, The White House, 24 January 1968, Washington DC, National Archives of Australia A1209, 1966/7413.
166. See McEwen *John McEwen: His Story*, p. 70.
167. Ibid.
168. Ibid., p. 71.
169. "Leadership still open: bid for a quick vote at today's Liberals meeting," *Australian Financial Review*, 9 January 1968.
170. See recent article: "Statue of caretaker prime minister and long-serving Country Party leader John McEwen planned for parliamentary zone," *Canberra Times*, 19 August 2020.
171. McEwen, *John McEwen:His Story*, p. 78.
172. Adam Smith, Introduction in *Wealth of Nations*, Books IV-V, 1999, first published 1776, Penguin Classics, London, p. 5.
173. Michelle Grattan, *The Conversation: 2020 the Year that Changed us*, Thames and Hudson, 2020, p. 9.
174. McEwen, *John McEwen: His Story*, p. 78.
175. Greg Sheridan, "Coronavirus: As we slowly reopen, migrants must top our agenda," *The Australian*, 19 November 2020.
176. Romy Wasserman and Alan Gamlen, "Literature Review: Policy that encourages population to relocate to regional areas," Hugo Centre for Migration and Population Research, Page

Research Centre, 2020.
177. McEwen, *John McEwen: His Story* p. 82
178. Ibid., p. 85.

ACKNOWLEDGEMENTS

This book could not have been written without the Country Party, and its people- a political movement that is now over a century old, that continues to evolve. So to the Country Party of old, The Nationals of now, thank you for providing me ballast, grit and inspiration.

From our membership, to our MPs thank you for standing up. In particular Victorian Nationals grass root members and Stanhope locals, Frank Stephens and Murray Buzza; former state Nationals MPs Billy Baxter and Pat McNamara; McEwen's ministerial protegees in federal parliament Peter Nixon, Ian Sinclair and Doug Anthony through his son and current president of the Nationals, Larry Anthony. All the Nationals leadership and Deputy Prime Ministers, for sharing their thoughts on the legacy that Black Jack left our Party and John Anderson for his candid thoughts on economic matters.

Thank you also to John Howard, former Prime Minister for his delightful and interesting discussion of trade, protectionism, Menzies and McEwen's partnership amongst other topics. A special thank you to Bruce Lloyd who succeeded McEwen in the seat of Murray and provided insightful reflections on the man from both a local and national perspective.

To the National Party historians Paul Davey and Andrew Black, thank you for filling in the gaps and from your own publications providing me with the springboard for further research and ideas. Paul, your contribution to documenting the history of our Party over a long time is so significant. We as a Party really need to make sure all your books are in the federal parliamentary library as the current Country Party, Nationals collection does not adequately reflect our Party's contribution to the political history of Australia.

Appreciation and gratitude to my research assistant and collaborator on this project, the talented A. L. McManus a young man with a very bright future.

To my small group of significant others for their advice (whether sought and not), long weekends, better words, included phrases, brutal editing and copious coffee.

My staff for their patience and assistance with strange requests they fulfilled with diligence and curiosity, from word clouds to correcting citations.

Also thank you to the Australian Parliamentary Library, in particular Juli Tomaras who assisted with key material and research.

Thank you, John and Wendy Stone for hosting tea at their home in Sydney and a delightful chat about Max Newton, McMahon and Oxbridge.

The economic professors Drysdale and Anderson who gave of their time freely with careful and considered views I very much appreciated.

To the celebrated Paul Kelly, whose political insights and reflections I increasingly lean on- thank you for our frank interview and for agreeing to launch my book.

To my editor and dear friend Dr. Scott Prasser, thank you for trusting me with this project. An untested author, some would say a reluctant writer who stopped studying history in mid secondary school is asked to write a 'biography' on the most significant of Country Party prime ministers. Thank you for recognising that to develop a written collection of Australian conservative politicians, the Country Party men (in the main) deserve to be rightfully recognised and better understood. Hopefully my small contribution can stimulate renewed interest in our collective conservative history and contribution to the Australian political narrative.

John McEwen

INDEX

Abbott, Tony, Prime Minister, 13
Abe, Shinzo, Prime Minister, 13
Aboriginal Australians, 9
Agrarianism, 53
Anderson, John, politician, 30
Anglophilia, 71, 76
Anthony, Doug, politician, 65, 94, 96, 106, 109
Aristotle, 84
Associated Chamber of Manufactures, 31
Australian Broadcasting Corporation (ABC), 90, 91
Australian Financial Review, 101, 133
Australian Industry Development Corporation, 98
Australian manufacturing, 14, 17, 19, 21-22, 30, 31, 85, 138, 140, 143-146
Australian population, 22, 24, 31-32, 38, 81, 85, 142-144, 146-147
Ballarat, Victoria, 57
Ballard, B.C., public servant, 80-82
Barton, Edmund, Prime Minister, 8
Baxter, Bill, politician, 92
Bendigo, Victoria, 45
Bjelke-Petersen, Joh, politician, 93
Black, Andrew, historian, 15
Brazil, 17
Brennan, Frank, politician, 63, 71
Bretton Woods, 19
Brisbane, Queensland, 78
Bruce, Stanley, prime minister, 69
Buick, 47, 126
Bull, Tom, politician, 19
Buzza, Murray (resident), 47

Cambridge University, 69, 101
Cameron, Archie, politician, 51, 73, 83
Canberra, 8, 16, 27, 37, 43, 45, 47, 49, 51-52, 56-58, 60-62, 79, 88-91, 97-99, 101, 106-110, 114-115, 128-130, 141-145
Casey, Richard, governor-general, 69, 80, 103
Catholicism, 71
Charolais, 47
Chifley, Ben, prime minister, 8, 22, 90, 100, 138
Chilgala, Victoria, 16, 45-47, 106, 126
Chiltern, 37-40, 45
Chipp, Don, politician, 102
Churchill, Winston, prime minister, 78
Coalition (Australian politics), 55-56, 58, 61, 63-66, 73-74, 100-112, 116, 119-120, 123, 133, 141, 146
Cold War, 117
COVID-19, 135, 139, 144
Crawford, John, public servant, 25-27, 29, 72-73, 92
Curtin, John, prime minister, 8, 11, 52, 70-71, 77
Dandenong, 43
Davey, Paul, author, 131
de Gaulle, Charles, president, 77-79, 81-84
Deakin, Alfred, Prime Minister, 20
Department of Trade and Industry, 97, 115
Drysdale, Peter (academic), 29
dumping (trade), 19, 20
Dunstan, AA, politician, 55, 57-58, 61

Duntroon military college, 43
Echuca, Victoria, 91
Elizabeth II, queen, 129
Evans, Bruce, politician, 58
Evatt, H.V., politician, 9, 12
Fadden, Arthur, prime minister, 47, 66, 77, 138
Farming, 23, 35-37, 45, 48, 72, 96
Fiji, 77
Fischer, Tim, politician, 66
Fonterra, 50
Forde, Frank, Prime Minister, 9
foreign investment, 98, 130, 137-138, 146
France, 78-80, 82-84
Fraser, Malcolm, Prime Minister, 12, 20, 66
Free Trade (economics), 13, 18-19, 21, 27, 42, 54, 59
Freemasonry, 55
Fremantle, WA, 52
French African colonies, 17
G20, 32
Gallipoli, Turkey, 23
General Agreement on Tariffs and Trade (GATT), 13-14, 16-19, 21, 30
Geneva, Switzerland, 16-17, 93
Gerard Henderson (journalist), 20
Gippsland, Victoria, 55, 70, 107
Girton Girls Grammar, 45
Golding, Peter, author, 9, 21, 24, 28-30, 54, 59, 93, 99
Gorton, John, prime minister, 33, 86, 109-113, 124-125, 131-133
Graham, B.D., academic, 48, 52, 54
Grattan, Michelle, journalist, 140
graziers, 21, 53-55
Greece, 17

Hasluck, Paul, politician, 25, 109, 112
Hawke, Bob, prime minister, 20, 113
Heath, Edward, politician, 128-129
Hirohito, emperor, 82
Hitler, Adolf, 75, 78-79, 81, 83
Ho Chi Minh City, 83
Holschiver, Bob (resident), 49
Holt, Harold, prime minister, 20, 33, 77, 93, 98-99, 101-108, 110, 112, 114, 116, 118, 121-122, 126-127
Hotel Canberra, 60, 114
Howard, John, prime minister, 20, 66
Hughes, Billy, prime minister, 47, 70, 77
Industrial Relations, 20, 143
Ireland, 39
Japan, 11-14, 16, 23-24, 26-27, 40, 77-82, 84, 97, 117, 122, 129 (note includes reference to "Japanese")
Japan Export Trade Organisation, 117
Johnson, Lyndon B., president, 40, 127-130
Keating, Paul, prime minister, 22
Kelly, Paul, Journalist, 15, 32, 64, 100-101, 108, 140
Kennett, Jeff, politician, 58
Keynesian economics, 25
Kings Cross, Sydney, 100
Korean War, 9, 64
Kyabram Butter Factory, 49
Labor Party, 12, 20-22, 42, 54-55, 58-59, 61-63, 65, 71, 75, 100
laissez-faire (economics), 136
Lang Labor, 61
Lawler, Peter, public servant, 106-107
Liberal Party, 21, 55, 58, 63-65, 86, 91, 93, 97-98, 100, 103-105, 108-112, 116, 123-125, 132-133
liberalisation (economics), 17

Index

Lloyd, Bruce, politician, 60
London, UK, 71-73, 81, 90, 114
Lyons, Joseph, prime minister, 56-57, 61-63, 69, 73
Macklin, Robert, press secretary, author, 70
McEwen, David (father), 39
McEwenism, 9-10, 14, 19, 22, 30, 32, 100, 135, 147
McLeod, Annie (wife), 45
McMahon, Billy, prime minister, 63-64, 96, 99-101, 103-105, 107-118, 122, 124-125, 132-133, 136
McNamara, Pat, politician, 25, 54
Melbourne, 39, 40-44, 49, 55, 57, 61, 63, 69, 113, 128-129, 148
Melbourne Cup, 61, 63
Melville, Leslie (public servant), 29
Menzies, Robert, prime minister, 8, 12, 20, 32-33, 41, 49, 51, 64-66, 69-74, 76-79, 81-83, 90, 93-96, 98, 103, 108, 121, 123-125, 133, 136, 138
Moss, George, politician, 57
Murdoch, Keith, businessman, 90
Nazism, 78
New Caledonia, 77-84
New Hebrides, 78, 80, 83
New South Wales, NSW, 21
New Zealand, 17-18, 128
Newton, Maxwell, journalist, 29, 31, 91, 100-101, 104-105, 113-118, 122
Nicaragua, 17
Nixon, Peter, politician, 15, 19, 24, 27, 58, 65, 87, 94-96, 101, 106-107, 109-110, 123
Noumea, New Caledonia, 78, 80-81, 83-84
Numurkah, Victoria, 74-75
Ottawa Agreement, 26, 29, 71, 99

Packer family, 114, 116, 125
Packer, Frank, 125
Page, Earle, prime minister, 56, 61-65, 73-75, 77, 108, 111, 141
Pakistan, 17
Papua New Guinea, 24
Paterson, Banjo, poet, 35, 54
patriotism, 70, 77
Pélcier, Georges, 79-81
Peru, 17
Port Lincoln, SA, 13
Porter, Amy Ellen (mother), 39
Porter, Nellie (grandmother), 40-42, 46
Presbyterianism, 39, 55
protection for all, 14, 21-22, 24, 28, 31, 118, 136
Protectionism (economics), 14, 20, 25, 30, 42, 54, 135, 140, 155
Queanbeyan, NSW, 51
Rattigan, Alf, Public Servant, 14, 29-32
Realism (International Relations), 16
Reid, Alan, journalist, 88
Robinson, Peter, journalist, 88
Roosevelt, F.D., president, 76, 78-80
Rupert Murdoch, businessman, 89-91, 116, 118, 125
Ryan, Peter, politician, 58
San Francisco, USA, 9
Scullin, James, prime minister, 61-62
Seneca, 69
Shann, Edward, economist, 25
Shepparton, Victoria, 92
Shorten, Bill, politician, 90
Sinclair, Ian, politician, 65-66, 94-96, 106-107, 123
Smith, Adam, economist, 100, 139
socialism (economics), 55
soldier settlers, 37, 48-49, 51 54, 56

South Africa, 17-18
South Pacific, 23
Spry Charles, public servant, 116, 122
St Kilda, Melbourne, 40
Stanhope, Victoria, 37, 44-47, 49-50
Stevens, Frank (resident), 46
Sun Tzu, 87
Sydney Morning Herald, 97, 117
Tariff Board, 14, 28-29, 31
tariffs, 13-19, 21, 24, 30, 72, 98-99, 101, 131, 137
Teese, Colin, academic, 15
The Age, 31
The Australian (newspaper), 89, 91, 98, 101, 116-117, 133
The Australian Democrats, 60, 102
The Country Party, 7, 10, 20-22, 28, 36, 42, 51-67, 74, 77, 83, 88-89, 91-92, 94, 103, 107-110, 112, 118-120, 123-124, 133, 138
The Department of Trade, 28, 97, 115, 145
The Great Depression, 23, 51, 71
The Kennedy Round, 17-18
'the Pledge', 57
The Western Front, 23
Thucydides, 11
Tokyo, Japan, 11, 13
Toyota, 13
Treasury, 27-29, 97-98, 101, 113-115
Truss, Warren, politician, 77
Twain, Mark, author, 51
United Australia Party, UAP, 56-57, 61, 65, 73-74, 108, 124
United Kingdom, UK, 27, 32, 69, 72-73, 130
United Nations, 9, 21
United States of America, USA, 9, 16-17, 27, 64, 76, 78-80, 84, 113-114, 127-128, 130-131, 137
Vichy regime, 78, 81-82
Victoria, 9, 21, 38, 41-42, 44, 48-49, 52-61, 74, 91, 120, 125
Vietnam War, 86, 117, 127-129, 131-132
Wangaratta, Victoria, 37, 40, 42
Ward, Russell, historian, 53
Westerman, Alan, public servant, 11, 25, 27-29, 117
Western Australia, 26, 91
wheat growers, 53-54, 72-76
White Australia policy, 9, 20
Whitlam, Gough, Prime Minister, 15, 29, 43, 136
Wilson, Harold, prime minister, 98, 128-129
Wirraway (plane), 24
Wood, Alan, journalist, 101
World Bank, 29, 114
World Trade Organisation, 19-20
World War I, 37, 43, 54, 70, 138
World War II, 13, 21, 32, 66, 71, 90, 106, 117, 124, 137-138, 142, 148
Yarralumla, 77, 107
Yass, NSW, 90

www.ingramcontent.com/pod-product-compliance
Lightning Source LLC
Chambersburg PA
CBHW061941220426
43662CB00012B/1989